Ecodence Publishing
Boulder, Colorado
www.ecodencebooks.com

First Edition: March 2011

Photographs are used with permission
Cover Art licensed: iStockPhoto.com

A Letter to U.S.Middle-ClassChristians

Daniel Burgin

> *"First they ignore you, then they ridicule you,*
> *then they fight you, then you win."*
>
> **- Mahatma Ghandi**

An Ecodence Publishing Book

A very special thank you to my most significant

other, Katia, for enduring 100's of hours of

research and discussion as I framed the argument

I wanted to make with this book.

I owe you a great debt of gratitude for enduring

my tireless fascination with politics.

My everlasting love and respect.

Now let's eat!

About the Author

In 1980 I voted for the first time as an adult. I was 21 years old. I went to the GOP convention in Dallas and sold campaign buttons for the Reagan/Bush campaign.

It was thrilling.

As a native Texan I had grown up believing in the Republican Party, in Conservative principles and economic theory. Over the course of my life, and as I have studied politics and economics, I have learned that the policies of the GOP are unsustainable, even illogical.

What I share with you in this open letter is what I have learned. We are being lied to by Republican politicians. They do not represent our best interests. Indeed it is easy to show that they in fact use us to gain and keep power - pretending to stand for what we believe while padding the pockets of business interests who funnel them millions in contributions - against the very basic good of those who vote them into office.

If you keep an open mind, and are a seeker of the truth, I believe you will see - at some point in your reading - that I am right.

Daniel Burgin
March, 2011

Foreword

"Let us, then, with courage and confidence pursue our own Federal and Republican principles, our attachment to union and representative government...entertaining a due sense of our equal right to the use of our own faculties, to the acquisitions of our own industry, to honor and confidence from our fellow-citizens, resulting not from birth, but from our actions and their sense of them; enlightened by a benign religion, professed, indeed, and practiced in various forms, yet all of them inculcating honesty, truth, temperance, gratitude, and the love of man; acknowledging and adoring an overruling Providence, which by all its dispensations proves that it delights in the happiness of man here and his greater happiness hereafter—with all these blessings, what more is necessary to make us a happy and a prosperous people?

Still one thing more, fellow-citizens—a wise and frugal Government, which shall restrain men from injuring one another, shall leave them otherwise free to regulate their own pursuits of industry and improvement, and shall not take from the mouth of labor the bread it has earned. This is the sum of good government, and this is necessary to close the circle of our felicities."

Thomas Jefferson
First Inaugural Address
March 4, 1801

Contents

Your beliefs as strategic fodder for the GOP

You are a middle-class American, a Christian with a reverence for the Bible and the teachings of Jesus Christ. You believe the Democrats in the federal government and perhaps many longtime Republicans are not listening to you. You believe the US Constitution is a document written following Christian principles, namely the Ten Commandments from the Old Testament. You generally believe that politicians are harming our society; perhaps you even believe that some politicians are destroying the fabric of our shared Christian values. You believe in, and perhaps even support the Tea Party. You believe that our country is immoral in the eyes of God if abortion is allowed to continue, if gays are allowed to marry, if military spending is curtailed - lessening US global power - a bad thing, you believe - since the US is a just and righteous country, created in the image of our Judeo-Christian God and our influence, political and military, around the world is an inarguable force for good.

These things you believe.

You may believe other things as well. You may believe that "Obamacare", as you might like to call it, is socialized medicine, a government takeover of the best health care system in the world. You may believe that the US Constitution was written by our Christian founders, God-fearing people like you. You may believe that our military will be weakened now that gays are allowed to serve openly in our armed forces. You may believe President Obama is not a Christian like you, but rather a secret Muslim. You may further believe that our President was not born in the US - making him constitutionally illegitimate. You may believe you are not a socialist (I will show you that you probably are and that this is probably a good thing). You may believe that our President, and indeed many Liberals are Socialists and don't believe in a free market economy. You may believe that if Republicans were put firmly in charge of our government and held to task by people like you, the US economy would flourish and our debts would subside, perhaps even disappear. Even if you don't fully believe the things in this paragraph, you have many conservative friends and colleagues who do believe these things.

You believe in these things and many others, and your beliefs are bolstered by what your GOP elected officials tell you - confirming the rightness of your beliefs.

If you could answer yes to some, perhaps much of the above declarations, you should read on. As I will show, you have been misled by people you trust who tell you they care about the social issues you care about - they don't - as we shall prove. If you care to keep an open mind, I'm confident you will see that you are being used to make rich Americans ever more so, and that this wealth is contributed to the rich from your pocket. This book will lay out facts and history to bolster the argument that you are being deceived. I believe that if you keep an open mind you will see the sometimes ugly truth and realize that you have been lied to, misled, manipulated by those pretending to represent you - when in reality they are working against your best interest - aggressively.

This book is a discussion of political strategies of conservative politicians, and their effects on the US economy and in general the well-being of our society. I know some of what I posit will be controversial, but I have taken care to support my views with facts, documents in many cases, and I am confident this view is logical and represents reasoned and defensible views on the subject. You may already be thinking I am wrong. On this we can agree, even now, one of us is right and one of us is not.

Most of us are too busy living our lives, working, raising our children, and even just relaxing to pay close enough attention to the details of what is happening, really happening in our government. In other words, we are easy prey for those who say one thing, but then disingenuously implement policies and laws that are driving toward an outcome completely different from their words and protestations. Instead of addressing what you believe in, the issues they campaign on, once in office they drive hard at outcomes that are deeply harmful to you, your family, and our countries future – as we shall see.

The aim of this book is to create a construct for understanding the purposeful divisiveness of our political discourse - a divisiveness that stimulates the fears and biases of the GOP voter base, distracted from the facts of what is happening by the business of our daily lives. This book is based on facts and data that show that the greatest threat to America's national health, both short-term and long-term, is the willful manipulation by some politicians - mostly conservatives - who are exploiting social issues of voters too busy working to notice the lies. These politicians purposefully and even masterfully ignite and feed the fire of fears, cultural biases, and religious hot buttons so they can gain our trust, attain official power and remain in power. We will examine all these issues and more, but more to the point, we will examine the fact that these issues are the gas in the GOP's manipulative and disingenuous electoral engine aimed at manipulating you, the Christian conservative right. All of this will be explored in more depth in this and upcoming chapters.

But wait, you may be saying, GOP politicians do work on social issues important to their Christian conservative constituency. Well, in a way. Let me explain. Once in power these conservative politicians do indeed attempt (and almost always fail) to support the social, religious, and cultural issues of their constituents, but all the while in office are pressing an economic agenda that is harmful to their middle-class constituents, and that is at the very heart of our undoing. Their economic agenda harms most the wallets of those middle-class voters who elected these lawmakers. It is a tragic game, played by ambition-driven politicians, who disingenuously play on the fears and biases of their God-fearing constituents who are too busy working to see the truth. They lie to the very people who vote for them, to get elected. Once in office, they gain the platform and power to press their illogical and harmful (as I will show) economic policies to favor their corporate sponsors and benefactors - and harm the middle class.

You are being used to make corporations and wealthy individuals ever wealthier. This is a zero sum game - as their actions make you less powerful, poorer, and more likely to fall into financial ruin.

This is manipulative, disingenuous, dangerous, and is counter to almost all reasoned analysis of what is good and healthy for America. But worst of all, I will show that in ignoring the economic needs of the middle class in favor of business interests, the obvious singular approach of the GOP, these conservative politicians are pursuing an outcome that is ultimately bad for all; bad for those who vote for the Right on the grounds of culture war issues without doubt, but even destructive (self-destructive) to these politicians and their corporate donors.

I mentioned earlier that conservative politicians attempt and fail to implement conservative social agenda's (outlaw abortion, outlaw gay marriage, press for even more unimpeded gun rights, bringing God into the US government, etc). Why do they fail? Is it perhaps because they want to fail? Perhaps not, but imagine if all these conservative desires were fully supported by our laws. Wouldn't GOP politicians then lose the social agenda hooks that allow them to support culture war issues to get votes? During the most recent Bush Administration, when the GOP held majorities in The White House, the Senate, the House, and the US Supreme Court, why didn't abortion become illegal? Why weren't the Ten Commandments allowed to be displayed in all Federal Courts? Why weren't Social Security and Medicare/Medicaid terminated for good? It's an interesting problem to ponder - and ponder we will in upcoming chapters.

First, I want to establish the logical reasoning behind my conclusion that the GOP's financial theories are wrong-headed, unworkable, and ultimately deeply destructive to a healthy US economy and society, destructive to most of those who elect them, and even eventually deeply destructive to themselves and their wealthy individual backers and wealthy corporate benefactors. I will show that conservative economic theories are illogical, demonstrably so, and further I will show that if they are implemented or left unchecked, will drive us into extinction as a great financial player in the world economy, and destroy the voice of freedom and human dignity that is America's great gift to the world.

For more than a century, Americans have believed in a capitalist free market, and further that if our markets are largely freed from government oversight and protected from any undue tax burdens, that this is the best means upon which to build a wealthy nation. In this construct, anyone could become fabulously wealthy based upon the merit of their own ideas and hard work. This is a universally held belief, provably true, and is the basis of America's great financial wealth and power.

A brief example of the power of free markets and entrepreneurship. I have a friend; let's call him Steve (not his name). In 1999 he noticed a conceptual opportunity in the online auction space, a hole if you will in the business models of eBay and Amazon - both working furiously at the time to attract users to their online auction sites for used retail goods. His concept was simple. What if he could build a website where consumers could sell their used items, books, music CD's, DVD's etc. that they no longer wanted? But his model had a twist.

Rather than used items being subjected to auction dynamics where prices are set by the highest bidder, used items for sale would be priced at half price for those items in good condition, and priced downward from there if items were more heavily used. For instance, a book bought at retail price for $30, still in excellent condition could be sold for $15. Users simply entered the ISBN number listed on the book, an image of the book would appear, and the item was listed. Simple, and effective and filled a conceptual hole in the online auction space.

Steve hired a co-founder programmer, who started to build a prototype, and Steve began talking to investors about the idea. In the summer of 1999 they raised a relatively small amount of capital, a few million dollars, launched the site, and began to operate the business and attract consumers wishing to sell their items not in an auction, but for a fair half price. In less than a year, eBay noticed his site, saw that it filled a hole in their business model, and negotiations began. Shortly thereafter, Steve and his small team of employees and investors sold the business for more than $300M. Since investors usually take 40-50% ownership in the business, Steve and his small founder group made a tidy $150M for themselves in about a year. And since this was income from a stock investment, it's highly likely the government considered this capital gains income, not wages, and taxed the income at only 15%, rather than 39%, the top regular income rate at the time.

The free market is a gold mine for rewarding good ideas that are well executed. This opportunity is open to all Americans and is a byproduct of our free market. Clearly, free markets are a powerful idea and a gift to Americans.

However, unharnessed capitalism is not universally a good thing. For a capitalist economy to thrive there must be a large and functioning middle-class, with lots of disposable income to spend and drive the economy - buying the products and services of those who create them (entrepreneurs). Pure capitalist economies do not exist. All capitalist economies are some combination of free, unfettered capitalism and socialist policies that protect those that fail to thrive (programs like Social Security, Medicare, Medicaid, Universal Health care... just to name a few in the US). This capitalist economy is further balanced by a government which can tax, which has oversight to protect the common good (the overall economy, financial markets, the environment, worker's rights, etc.) and the teeth to enforce substantive, behavior modifying penalties on those who flaunt regulations.

From a purely conservative ideological perspective, those who "fail to thrive", as I put it, are on their own. It is their fault if they are dumb or lazy enough to fail having the great luck to be born in the world's most successful economy. Further conservative ideologues will argue that in a fair and efficient economy, why should the wealthy pay for the poor? It's fundamentally unfair, right? This is a matter of ideological purity and not a serious argument in my view. Unfortunately, the real world doesn't function in a pure way - it's messy and sub-optimal. We have to accept that pure capitalism doesn't work - however much conservative ideologues would like to believe it would. Mixed economies of capitalism and "practical socialism" are the only model anywhere in the world – there are no purely capitalistic economies, and for goodf reason. As former aide to US Senator Daniel Patrick Moynihan, and now MSNBC commentator, Lawrence O'Donnell states, "mixed economies of capitalism and "practical socialism" are the only workable free market model. As a matter of fact, all capitalist societies in the world are some mix of capitalism and socialism".

As to this idea of ideological purity; it would be nice if everyone could simply flap their arms and fly, or close their eyes and teleport across the country or the world - after all this would be a "highly efficient" means of travel. Call it "Ideologically Pure Travel". Wishing it doesn't make it so. It is simply intolerable, within well-defined boundaries of relative fairness, for those who "fail to thrive" to be subjected to a life of misery, hunger, and homelessness. It's bad for our society, and bad for our economy. Some "practical socialism" that supports reasonable means of stopping poverty that does not overly harm innovation and capitalism is required, is ethical, and is unavoidable. As Lawrence O'Donnell states, "he [O'Donnell] was a socialist because he supported programs such as Medicare and Social Security -- which are, he said, explicitly socialistic at heart. He described Medicare as "a socialist idea whose time had come in a capitalist society." Moreover, he said, everyone who supports such programs is supporting socialism. O'Donnell further quoted economist Milton Friedman's famous maxim that "we are all Keynesian's now," and adopted it for himself: "we are all socialists now." (Highly recommended video if you disagree with this point Lawrence O'Donnell[1]).

The business-biased and middle-class harming policies of the GOP cannot be allowed to continue. It will be the undoing of our economy - this seems entirely obvious, doesn't it? I think it does. Still not convinced, read on. There's much more to convince you.

If the GOP were to fully get its way, the course they would steer would quickly become unsustainable. For instance, cutting taxes for the wealthy under the provably false premise that the wealthy are job creators. For every dollar in tax cuts for the wealthy, less than 10 cents is returned to the market and creates jobs; this according to the non-partisan Congressional Budget Office,. Contrast that with the fact that extending unemployment benefits contribute 70 cents of every dollar invested back into the market. Each percentage point better these numbers rise, increases market demand for goods and services, and therefore creates jobs. Stunningly, simply extending unemployment benefits, among many other better choices than lowering taxes on the wealthy, is 7 times more effective than extending the so-called Bush Tax Cuts for the wealthy. (Congressional Budget Office[2])

The data shows that only a very small percentage, less than 2%, of wealthy individuals create jobs. Most jobs are created today by entrepreneurs in their late 20's and early 30's, and they are certainly not wealthy. The GOP has been very successful in allowing the wealthy to become ever more so, at the expense of balancing that outcome with sustaining the middle class. Imagine a country of struggling middle class workers in the millions, many currently unemployed, trying to keep their homes, send their children to college, pay for heat, buy food and clothing. Struggle as they might they continue to borrow at unsustainable rates to keep up, falling deeper and deeper into peril - sound familiar? If too many Americans fall into this struggle, who will buy the products and services of entrepreneurs - new and old - that drive growth, sustain government through consumption tax revenue to fund the maintenance of our nation's roads, bridges, highways, train systems, schools - the engines of capitalism?

It's easy to see isn't it? Fewer and fewer in the middle class will maintain their important consumption as their struggle deepens. If the top 1% of wage earners in America are allowed to own 40% or even 50% of the nation's wealth, that is the path we're inexorably on if the GOP gets its way, America's economy will cease to function, companies will fail as middle-class consumer demand weakens, tax revenues will dissipate, and we will slowly fail as a country - likely taking the rest of the world with us into economic hell.

Furthermore, if social safety nets are dismantled, programs like Unemployment Insurance for instance, designed to sustain families in their homes during inevitable economic downturns in our economy; affected families will cease to participate in the economy at all. This set of events will further exacerbate the stagnation of our economy. A vicious cycle that will lead to a spiraling down into economic death.

Additionally, the GOP is constantly pushing to lower corporate taxes. While the US corporate tax rate is higher than many countries, the GOP has been very successful in undermining this tax rate with exceptions. The US corporate tax code is so ripe with loopholes that many Fortune 500 companies pay no taxes at all. According to Forbes magazine, no liberal rag, "Some of the world's biggest, most profitable corporations enjoy a far lower tax rate than you do--that is, if they pay taxes at all. The most egregious example is General Electric. [In 2009] the conglomerate generated $10.3 billion in pretax income, but [because of loopholes in US Tax Code] ended up owing nothing to Uncle Sam. In fact, it recorded a tax benefit of $1.1 billion". (Forbes Magazine[3])

On personal incomes, according to NY Times conservative columnist Nicholas Kristof, our transfer of wealth from the middle class to the wealthy has reached insane levels. Kristof writes,

"...the richest 1 percent of Americans now take home almost 24 percent of income, up from almost 9 percent in 1976. As Timothy Noah of Slate noted in an excellent series[4] on inequality, the United States now arguably has a more unequal distribution of wealth than traditional banana republics like Nicaragua, Venezuela and Guyana." Kristof continues, "C.E.O.'s of the largest American companies earned an average of 42 times as much as the average worker in 1980, but 531 times as much in 2001. Perhaps the most astounding statistic is this: From 1980 to 2005, more than four-fifths of the total increase in American incomes went to the richest 1 percent."

Clearly conservative economic policies are enriching their wealthy individual and corporate benefactors at the expense, and directly from the wallets of the middle class - whose incomes have been stagnant for almost 20 years. (Nicholas Kristof, NY Times[5])

Given this situation, who in their right mind would continue to give tax breaks to the wealthy? Isn't 24% of our wealth for the top 1% enough?

Who would want to dismantle social safety nets right when the risk is increasing?

Who would want to lower corporate tax rates on companies who have had their richest quarters ever, and many pay low tax rates as a result of GOP loopholes, some paying no tax at all?

This is economic suicide.

But this is exactly what Republicans want; static taxes on the middle class offering no growth in incomes, little or no taxes on corporations, rollbacks on all social safety nets like Unemployment Insurance, Social Security, Medicare, Medicaid, and Katie-bar-the-door, don't ever let (gasp) low-income Americans have access to free-market managed health care.

What the GOP pejoratively calls "Obamacare" is just that, free-market managed universal health care, which lowers our deficits substantially over time according to the non-partisan Congressional Budget Office (CBO).

The CBO also forecasts that repealing the Affordable Care Act would increase deficits[6] by $210 billion in the first decade and by about $813 billion over the period 2012-2021.

More can be done, and will be done to bend the cost curve downward in upcoming health care legislation (assuming the ideologically pure GOP lawmakers, fighting against what is in every ones interests with their repeal nonsense, is removed from the US House of Representatives and more rational lawmakers preside), but the bill is a good start - despite lies from leadership on the Right. GOP politicians and pundits have railed about non-existent "Death Panels" meeting to do a cost-benefit analysis on treating grandma or letting her die (nonsense, created from whole cloth and propagated by prime manipulators like Sarah Palin and Newt Gingrich), lies about "Government takeover of Health care" and other such lies to further stimulate the already fearful GOP voter base, working too hard to pay close enough attention to see they are railing against their own best interests.

Did you see the anger in town hall meetings in the summer of 2010 with fearful GOP voters screaming at their elected representatives about death panels? It was frightening. Clearly these people believed the lies they had been told. They believed their health decisions were going to be made in some backroom by a team of bureaucrats. It would be funny were it not so tragically harmful to a rational discourse. It reminds me of that character played by the late Gilda Radner on Saturday Night Live, who rants uncontrollably on some topic she clearly misunderstands, and when corrected meekly replies, "Oh, never mind".

On taxes, it is such standard Republican talking point strategy now, that GOP lawmakers seem to have tax cut Turret's Syndrome, wherein their answer to every crisis is "cut taxes". It's like that chiropractor joke. No matter what ails you, he'll "crack your bones", as comedian Eddie Izzard parodies. "You have a backache; he'll crack your bones. Have diphtheria; he'll crack your bones".

For Republicans, it goes like this: Economy going down? "Cut Taxes". Economy going up? "Cut Taxes". It's illogical and misguided. Worse, it's unsustainable. Taxes in the US are now lower than they've been since the 1950's (USA Today, Tax bills in 2009 at lowest level since 1950[7]). We simply can't cut taxes and operate our economy.

But wait, you've been told by prominent Republicans like current House Speaker John Boehner that "we don't have a revenue problem (taxes), we have a spending problem in the Federal government". Perhaps, but what would you cut and not imperil the critical buying power of the middle class?

The standard answer to that question for Republicans like you seems easy - or is it? GOP pundits and leaders say "cut social programs, which make up 2/3rds of our spending".

Seems logical right? But which programs and how? When surveyed, even Tea Party Conservatives, the most virulent backers of decreased federal spending as the answer, don't want these social programs cut - and with good reason. They're all largely middle class, and if disaster strikes they are up the creek without a paddle and they know it.

According to the NY Times,

"...despite their push for smaller government, [Tea Party backers] think that Social Security and Medicare are worth the cost to taxpayers". (NY Times, Tea Party Poll finds backers wealthier and more educated[8]).

Still, we have to curtail the growth of these programs as the population ages and the workforce shrinks - which is occurring now as the baby boom generation retires.

There are means to reduce growth rates without unnecessary risk to these safety nets.

Let's take Social Security as an example. Social Security is solvent for about the next 30 years.

However, it is growing fast and within 5-7 years or so, the output will surpass the income. That is more people will be collecting than paying into the program as the workforce shrinks and the retirement community grows.

Simple changes, like increasing the retirement age when benefits could be gathered could be slowly increased over time, moving it from 65 years of age, to 67, and then some years later to 69.

With our expanding life spans this would not be terribly problematic for most workers, and for those where it is problematic, some exceptions could be made. For instance, for those in manual labor jobs.

Additionally, a means test could be applied. People who pay into the program but earn more on average than $250,000/year in their last 10 years of employment are unlikely to need Social Security dollars in retirement.

Do millionaires and billionaires really need these dollars to remain active consumers in a healthy economy? No. These and other practical adjustments to Social Security are being discussed and should be implemented to make this program sustainable for many more decades.

But what else could we cut. Military spending is at the top of my list. The US deploys thousands of soldiers around the world to protect our "interests", mostly petroleum, at great cost to the US, and no cost to the countries who benefit from our troop presence. Simply charging these countries for US troops is a good start. I'll speak more to other options in later chapters, but military spending cuts is a good place to start; the US can no longer afford to be the free policeman for the world and other emerging economies must step up. Of course the GOP opposes this idea. Surely you're not surprised.

Here's another example of government waste which should be harvested for maintaining our free markets. The richest industry in the history of the world is the oil business. GOP candidates have reaped millions in contributions from oil companies over the past decade. These oil companies have pushed these financed lawmakers for massive tax breaks and subsidies. Why would the US subsidize the richest industry in history? It makes no sense.

"We're giving tax breaks to highly profitable companies to do what they would be doing anyway," said Sima J. Gandhi, a policy analyst at the Center for American Progress, a liberal research organization. "That's not an incentive; that's a giveaway."

Many Republican lawmakers are so deeply in the pockets of the oil industry that their behavior is transparently submissive and lacking any true "common good" leadership. During the British Petroleum (BP) oil spill in the Gulf of Mexico in 2010, President Obama proposed to the BP CEO that a fund be established, financed by BP that would be set aside to make sure the company quickly and efficiently repaid the communities in the region for the clean-up and the financial harm caused by the companies' negligence. During a Senate hearing, Senator Joe Barton, Republican of Texas, actually apologized to the CEO of BP, claiming he was 'embarrassed', for the establishment of this fund - which the BP CEO had agreed to without resistance as the right thing to do to speed recovery post-spill. It's obscene.

According to the NY Times, there are nine categories of subsidies to this already wealthy industry, which has dozens of companies posting billion dollar profits every calendar quarter. These nine categories are: Intangible drilling costs, Deductions for tertiary injectants, Percentage depletion allowance, Passive investments, Domestic manufacturing tax deduction, Geological and geophysical expenditures, foreign tax credit, Enhanced oil recovery credit, and Marginal well production. Doesn't that sound like we're padding the substantially profitable books of oil companies with taxpayer money? Right, it sounds like that because that is exactly what it is - a giveaway as thanks for political contributions. President Obama has proposed ending these subsidies. Of course the oil-industry GOP lawmakers are deeply indebted to the oil industry for their contributions, so the GOP opposes ending these nonsense subsidies.

But adjustments in social programs, reduction in military spending to protect oil interests, and nonsense industry subsidies are not enough. Investment is also required. Just as the federal government created the Internet in the 1960's, which led to one of the largest expansions in GDP in our lifetimes as the consumer web grew from this government investment, other strategic investments must be made. One idea in this category has been proposed by NY Times Thomas Friedman in countless articles. His idea is US investment in a green economy. Friedman argues, correctly, that this would not only spur economic growth (perhaps even a boom), but would also end our dependence on foreign oil, minimize the power of what he calls "Petrocracies" (Saudi Arabia, Libya, Egypt, etc) and all these US "interests" are no longer very interesting, and not worth the troop costs. (NY Times, As Oil Industry Fights a Tax, It Reaps Subsidies[9]) (Center for American Progress, Eliminating Tax Subsidies for Oil Companies10) (NY Times Friedman: The Energy Harvest11) (NY Times Friedman: If Not Now, When?12)

Clearly we have to rein in spending, decrease military expenditures we can no longer afford, stop subsidizing the most profitable industry of all time, the oil industry, a giant giveaway and a massive waste of precious tax revenue. And we must make reasonable adjustments to social programs to balance our budgets.

We must live within our means.

But, what are our means? Simple, tax revenues. Fairly taxing corporations and wealthy individuals. Does anyone really believe that GE should pay no taxes in 2009 during banner earnings, and indeed should get a $1.1B tax refund? Does anyone really believe that the wealthy would crumple under a "massive" 3 percent tax increase as proposed by President Obama - recession or not? Surely the wealthy would continue to be wealthy. Of course.

Seriously. A modest increase in taxes on the wealthy from 36% to 39% (as President Obama proposes) would not harm the wealthy, would not harm job creation (despite the factually unsupported arguments to the contrary by Conservative officials), and would increase our "means"; making it easier to balance budgets.

According to Nicholas Kristof of the NY Times again,

"[Under Obama's tax proposal], the richest 0.1 percent of taxpayers would get a tax cut of $61,000 from President Obama. They would get $370,000 from Republicans, according to the nonpartisan Tax Policy Center. And that provides only a modest economic stimulus, because the rich are less likely to spend their tax savings. On tax breaks for the wealthy, who remember are already richer than ever, now owning 24% of our incomes, don't need tax breaks, rarely create new jobs, and will not be harmed by this increase. At a time of 9.6 percent unemployment, wouldn't it make more sense to finance a jobs program? For example, the money could be used to avoid laying off teachers and undermining American schools". Or, invest in R&D innovations to drive a green economy, reducing our dependence on foreign oil, reduce our military expenditures and country subsidies to maintain stability in oil rich dictatorships, and spur job growth. The benefits are endless.

Indeed. As an aside, it heartens me that reasonable, logical commentators like Kristof still exist. They feel like a threatened species off in some corner awaiting extinction of late, as the increasingly conservative lunatic fringe of the GOP takes more and more control and targets moderate Republicans for upcoming elections. The far right calls these moderate GOP lawmakers "RINOs" an acronym for "Republicans In Name Only". It seems compromise and balance is not favored by our countrymen on the Right.

It is upon this shifting sand of fantasy economic ideology and draconian and misguided policy that conservative politicians now operate with increasing fervor. Allowing the GOP more power in our government, where they will lower taxes even more, allow corporations to continue pay no taxes, even get refunds, expand military spending, refuse to stop subsidizing already rich industries, deny investment in new growth sectors, and kill off important, reasonable social safety nets - is a recipe for disaster. The best indicator of future behavior is past behavior. Do we really need another GOP majority to see that trickle-down economics really is "voodoo economics", as George H.W. Bush called it, and that the GOP is NOT the fiscally responsible party, but are slaves to their corporate interests?

I will expand more on economic theories that have proven effective in later chapters, but a short taste of the latter now.

One of the most demonstrably provable strategies for managing economic growth is Keynesian economics in its various incarnations and updates. Keynesian economics is a wildly unpopular theory among conservative and libertarian ideologues - but demonstrably effective using historical facts and a policy that responsible Democrats have more or less followed, to great economic effect in recent times.

Generally speaking, the approach of John Maynard Keynes posited in his economic theory that the Federal government should invest, even incur debt in economic downturns, but must be disciplined to pay down this investment debt during economic upswings. Something generally followed by recent Democratic presidents, but not generally followed by GOP presidents.

Truly the GOP is NOT the fiscally responsible party. The numbers don't lie. MSNBC's The Rachel Maddow points out this phenomenon[13] and in the image below, graphing how,

"The myth of 'tax and spend' Democrats somehow being fiscal idiots while Republicans and conservatives are best trusted with budgets, is statistically untrue".

Maddow goes on to point out this fact about many GOP elected officials in recent memory, "People around the country need to realize - Republicans primary focus is on enhancing the power and influence of corporate America and the wealthy elite while growing their own [political] power.

To vote Republican is to vote against your own self interest for the vast majority of Americans".

Somehow conservative middle-class voters never seem to realize we are cutting our own throats

The Rachel Maddow Show, MSNBC

Republican presidents (like Reagan [189% debt growth] and George W Bush [89% debt growth]) have spent us into debt during their terms (see Maddow chart above) - growing the national debt at often twice the pace of their Democratic presidential counterparts.

They grow the debt during their terms at a staggering pace; then Democratic Presidents (Clinton [42% debt growth] after Reagan and Obama [TBD] after Bush) come in, invest in the US Economy and in the case of Clinton, despite increasing the debt, his administration even created a financial surplus from tax revenues.

One can argue cause and effect here (Clinton had the benefit of the Internet boom), but such booms are themselves the offspring of government investment. The Internet was created by, you guessed it, DARPA[14] - a government agency.

Investment in "Green technologies" could, one could argue will, spur a new growth economy - and hundreds of entrepreneurs with millions of employees.

A green economy investment is the answer - not flogging the middle class and giving gifts to the wealthy - who are wealthier than ever already.

This is my view, I believe it is supported by history and facts, and is the basis for my upcoming discussion on GOP political election strategy.

A strategy that brings their damaging policies into power on the backs of working people misled and manipulated against their own self-interest by the fervor of their fears, biases, and passions for religious, cultural, and race-driven social agendas.

The GOP would take us down a path which only prolongs our inability to have economic growth - fueled by a strong middle class - that is sustainable for decades.

**The numbers game behind GOP
strategies to manipulate voters**

America is a diverse country - but economically less so than you might think and growing less diverse everyday as the share of incomes moves at a dizzying pace toward the wealthy, and away from the middle-class. This creates two distinct classes: the very wealthy, and everyone else. If you're very wealthy, you're probably Republican. After all, GOP policies keep you getting richer by the day without effort on your part, other than your vote. If you're "everyone else" and not wealthy, why are you a Republican? The safe bet is social, religious, or cultural issues - most likely all related to your belief in Christianity. More on this in this chapter, but first, economics.

The vast majority of Americans grow poorer everyday - through inflation, stagnate wages, and government policy. We talked about this phenomenon before - remember this fact: The richest 1 percent of Americans now take home almost 24 percent of income, up from almost 9 percent in 1976 and from 1980 to 2005, more than four-fifths of the total increase in American incomes went to the richest 1 percent. Many among the rich see the insanity in keeping taxes so low on the wealthy[15]. This can't continue, and indeed must be reversed if our economy is to survive.

"There's class warfare, all right. **But it's my class- the rich class- that's making war, and we're winning."** I'm a conscientious objector.

—Warren Buffet

The power of the US economy, as discussed earlier, is the innovation-friendly financial environment that encourages and rewards successful entrepreneurship.

Think about innovations that you use everyday - even take for granted. Computers, PC/Mac operating systems, iPods, mobile phones, smart phones, automobiles, airplanes, Starbucks, CD players, Television, Satellite TV, DVD players, DVR's like Tivo, movies and music (the Entertainment industry), the Internet and its apps: Google, Yahoo!, Wikipedia, eBay, Facebook - all of these and many more were created in America.

American companies dominate the landscape of the world market for these inventions. Why is that?

It is the power of our free market.

As we discussed before, business interests within free markets are just part of the equation. For free markets to thrive, driven as they are by the simple power of supply and demand, another critical factor exists. Consumers, the "demand" side in the "supply and demand" equation are as important as supply, perhaps more so.
So who are consumers?

They're all of us, using our extra money, called disposable income by economists, to use the inventions companies create in the form of buying these companies' products.

To sustain a large middle-class of consumers - rampant business-oriented capitalism must be kept in check with consumer-oriented policy and protections. So how do we keep this critical equation balanced and in check?
Maintaining a healthy supply/demand balance is one of the key functions of government. Balancing the needs of business (the drivers of innovation - the supply side of the free market), and the needs of consumers (the demand side of the free market).

Trickle-down economics, wherein the government gives tax breaks to the wealthy, who in turn (a provably false theory) create businesses that benefit the rest of us by supplying jobs, is generally referred to as "supply-side economics". The GOP loves supply-side economics, even though it is a myth, as we have shown with facts, data, and not myth.

But back to this government balancing act between supply (business) and demand (consumers). If the government weights advantage too heavily to business, consumers have less money and demand dissipates. If the government weights advantage too heavily to consumers, businesses have less incentive and supply (innovation) declines. Both are problems, over-favoring business or over-favoring consumers are bad for our economy. Both. The balance must be maintained. So how are we doing on that?

For the last 30 years, the balance has been moving to the advantage of business, and to the detriment of consumers. This is not a controversial statement.

Some facts:

In the last 30 years, middle-class buying power has remained relatively constant, growing very little. Consumer buying power is a measure of what an average American makes in earnings balanced against what a dollar of those earnings will buy. Incomes must rise, as prices rise, or consumer buying power declines. Middle-class buying power has grown very slowly for 30 years. Incomes rise, but not fast enough to keep up with the rising cost of things (inflation). In the past 10 years consumer buying power is entirely flat. Most people are aware that inflation causes the cost of living (what you pay just to live in our country) to increase. The standard rate assumed by economists is about a 3% per year increase in cost of living. While this percentage fluctuates, it has been a relatively consistent standard for many years. As you can see, if the cost of living increases, but most peoples' incomes are not increasing at the same pace, a larger and larger share of what you earn goes to living expenses, and over time the disposable income, that income you use to buy new products and services goes down. There are other factors, but this is the important concept for our purposes.

But wait, you say, consumers are still buying companies' products and services. Company growth has continued. Right, but where did this money originate to buy these innovations, that disposable income? The answer is debt. Consumers in the US have been borrowing at unsustainable rates for a long time - climbing from 50% of the total size of the US market (called Gross Domestic Product, or GDP by economists) to near 300% of

GDP.

US Household debt 1946-2008

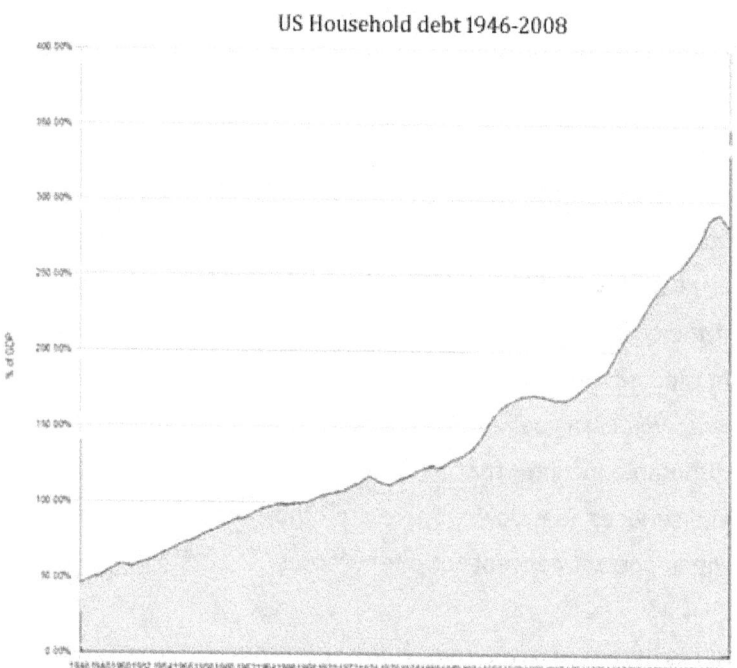

Wikipedia, US Consumer Debt 1946-2008

American middle-class consumers are out of disposable income, but borrowing at an increasing pace to keep consuming. Is that a good thing? Clearly not.

No one believes that consumers can continue borrowing at this rate, and indeed the dip at the end of the graph above is continuing downward. Consumers are borrowing less - a good thing - but the bad effects on the economy are also clear.

As consumers borrow less, they have less disposable income to spend on purchasing goods and services, and the less well companies do in profits.

The balance is out of whack, consumers are adjusting, and companies are shrinking. There are other factors, but this is the mega-trend.

As companies shrink, jobs are lost through layoffs, and for those not laid off, incomes are decreased through wage cuts, wage freezes, furloughs, worker benefits like health care, bonuses, and investments decreases.

Supply (companies) and demand (consumers) are intimately connected. To turn this around, consumer's incomes need to rise - giving them more income to spend, rather than debt, enabling consumers to continue to drive the economy and drive business profits.

Are consumer incomes growing?

No. A major lever the US government has to pull to manage this supply/demand balance are personal income tax structures that could put more income into the pockets of middle-class consumers and spur consumer spending growth. And giving more money to middle-class consumers stimulates overall economic growth, as middle-class consumers mostly spend the extra money.

So, are tax incentives doing that?

No, not really. While the so-called Bush Tax Cuts gave middle-class consumers some relief, the vast majority of the tax benefit, and therefore the real money, went to the wealthy.

Surely you're not surprised, after all Bush is a Republican who didn't end gay marriage, but did succeed in making the rich, far richer. The current tax structure, as a result of the Bush Tax Cuts, is heavily weighted toward the wealthy.

Remember, under President Obama's tax proposal (which was defeated by Republicans), we would have seen cuts for everyone, even the wealthy. For instance, under Obama's proposal everyone would get a break on the earnings up to $250,000. Obama's plan called for the richest 0.1 percent of taxpayers to get an average tax cut of $61,000.

Extending the Bush Tax Cuts (which were extended for 2 more years, as Republicans insisted) would get $370,000 from this Republican plan extension, according to the nonpartisan Tax Policy Center. $370,000 on average for already wealthy individuals! And during the second worst fiscal crisis in our history!

And the data shows that almost all of this money, our money, goes right into wealthy people's savings accounts - creating no jobs at all. In the middle of a serious recession, that's crazy, right?

Middle-class incomes are going to stay flat, and wealthy people's incomes are going to continue to grow, at least for 2 more years as of this writing in early 2010. President Obama has pledged to end the Bush Tax Cuts in 2012, raising taxes on the wealthy and removing more than $300,000 from the pockets of the wealthiest 0.1 percent of Americans. Believe me, they can afford it. Their average income is more than $6M/year as reported by the Congressional Budget Office. Worse, wealthy individuals are much less likely to spend the extra money, putting those dollars back into the economy and growing business profits. Insanity. Greed for the wealthy from the GOP is ruling the day, not concern for middle-class incomes.

So why would GOP elected officials continue to drive tax cuts toward the wealthy in such proportion, rather than the middle-class. They claim it's about jobs. It's not, there are no data supporting this view. Saying that taxing the wealthy is "job killing" is a statistically provable lie, economists and even millionaires agree[16]. So what's really going on?

The answer is fairly easy to understand, although it has several parts and requires a bit of discussion of election history in the US. Let's dive in.

Early in the last century, Republican politicians saw a looming problem in electoral math. The middle-class was emerging in vast numbers. The New Deal[17], started under FDR in 1933 (and fought tooth-and-nail by most Republicans) was introduced to stimulate the economy after the worst economic depression in US history. The program funded huge numbers of infrastructure projects (building roads, railroads, bridges, tunnels, and much more). The result was many poor people climbing into the middle-class as they attained steady work at fair pay.

This "New Deal" had a stimulative effect on the overall economy as well. With this new and growing population of consumers, companies began to create, build, and innovate massive numbers of products and services - driving up corporate profits at a dizzying pace - and creating many more jobs to build, market, and sell their new products. Companies like GE, Proctor and Gamble, and many others emerged and began to record massive growth numbers, creating ever more middle-class consumers. The Democratic Party stood firm at the side of consumers, working people, and the poor. The Republicans had a problem of electoral math. How to attract large numbers of citizens to vote Republican, when many Americans were directly and positively impacted by the policies of Democrats?

The GOP languished in the minority for a long time after this - well into the late 1960's. The GOP had to create a strategy that would turn out voters for them, and convince voters that the business-friendly philosophies of the GOP were in the public best interests, and further convince voters to reject the consumer-friendly policies of the Democrats. With the numbers against them, what did they do?

An emerging politician at the time, Richard Nixon, well before he became US President, adopted a strategy (created by a GOP political strategist named Kevin Phillips). This strategy became known as "The Southern Strategy".
This from Wikipedia[18]: "The Southern strategy refers to the late-20th century Republican Party strategy of winning elections in Southern states by exploiting anti-African

American racism among Southern white voters and appealing to states' rights. Though the "Solid South" had been a longtime Democratic Party stronghold due to the Democratic Party's defense of slavery prior to the American Civil War and segregation for a century thereafter, many Southern Democrats were alienated from the party following the African American Civil Rights Movement, the signing of the Civil Rights Act of 1964 by Democratic President Lyndon B. Johnson, and desegregation."Wikipedia continues, The strategy was first adopted under future Republican President Richard Nixon in the late 1960s and continued through the latter decades of the 20th century under Presidents Ronald Reagan and George H. W. Bush. The strategy was successful in achieving its goals; it led to the electoral realignment of Southern states to the Republican Party, but at the expense of losing over 90 percent of black voters to the Democratic Party. As the 20th century came to a close, the Republican Party began actively pursuing black voters again, though with little success. During the 2000s decade, Republican National Committee Chairman Ken Mehlman formally apologized for his party's use of the Southern Strategy in the previous century, and Michael Steele later became the party's first African American chairman."

In the last 15 years or so the Southern Strategy, which aimed at attracting large numbers of disaffected southern white voters by stoking their racism, began to lose its effectiveness. A newer twist on this disingenuous strategy had to be devised and followed - as the GOP still had a numbers problem in elections with their business-friendly, consumer-harming policies and economic philosophies. So where did they turn?

Their focus became the Religious Right. This group of mostly white, southern voters had begun to lose the sting of their racism. After all, Michael Jordon, Sydney Poitier, and even Republican National Committee leader Michael Steele and hundreds of other public figures were black, very articulate, likable, and many of these famous black Americans were loved by millions of white Americans.

So what did mostly white, religious Conservatives have as a bias that could be exploited to turn them into solid GOP voters? The answer is ugly, but true. Social Issues, used to wage a bitter culture war against the Democrats.

GOP candidates began to tout their religious convictions, real or feigned, brandishing their piety for Christian values, so called family values - and against more liberal notions of equality for women, gays, and immigrants.

They screamed at political rallies about the insidious and destructive beliefs of Democrats, using the word "liberal" as if it were an "anti-God" slur on the very character of Democratic politicians and voters. Their arguments played on the very real biases of the religious right - who believe it against Christ to be homosexual, or for young men and women to live together outside of marriage, or to have sexual relations outside of marriage, or for abortions to be legalized in any circumstance (even rape or incest), and on and on.

GOP politicians began to stoke the flames of bias against the liberal social views of Democrats, and convince religious conservatives that to vote for Democrats, was to vote against the church, the family, and even to vote against God.

Just as the Southern Strategy played on the fears of white citizens against blacks, and turned out southern voters in large majorities for the GOP, the new "Religious Southern Strategy" of GOP politicians plays directly on the fears of the mostly white, Christian conservatives against those who think and believe differently than they do.

Like the original Southern "Black" Strategy, the new Southern
"Christian" Strategy has been equally effective, as it has
turned out large majorities of southern white Christians for
years - as a matter of fact, the entire South, once solidly
Democratic, is now a wholly owned subsidiary of the
Republican party, and can be counted on to respond with
GOP votes when fanned with the fears, biases, and hatreds of
the large majority of Christians who live there.

What is lost here? What is lost is that the GOP, once in
office, does not vote to implement real change for
the Christian Conservative social issues that got them
elected.
They may make a ruse of it, but no big changes ever occur -
as a matter of fact quite the opposite. The military policy of
"Don't Ask, Don't Tell", which allowed gays to serve in the US
Military as long as their sexual preference was not known,
has just been defeated - and with GOP support.

Even while failing to fulfill their Christian-inspired campaign
promises on social issues, the GOP does not vote to protect
the rights of everyday working voters - southern or
otherwise.

The GOP casts its lot with business interests - and votes to increase the wealth of corporations and wealthy individuals (who are, of course, also Republicans - no surprise).

The fervor of GOP candidates in campaigns for supporting the social issue positions of southern Christians gets them the votes time and again.

They get elected, and then quietly implement laws that harm the wallets of their own middle-class voter base and make mock efforts to reform social issues of their Christian electorate.

They hope you won't notice - and as elections near - they gear up the rhetoric anew, touting those reliable "Christian Conservative Family values" - to turn you out at the polls for them again and again. A vicious and deceptive cycle that harms the middle-class in easy to measure ways and accomplishes nothing on the culture war front for Christian voters.

Don't you notice? An example, in the 2000 campaign when George W. Bush was running for President for the first time, a large number of key conservative states suddenly had a ballot initiative that would outlaw gay marriage.

That initiative was conceived, written and forced onto the ballot by the GOP in important GOP states for the general election, and backed publicly by Bush.

Christian voters, who might not turn out to vote for the GOP otherwise, were whipped into a frenzy to vote 'yes' for making gay marriage illegal - and oh by the way - while you're at the polls, also vote for George W. Bush for his presidential bid - after all he was on TV endlessly touting his support for banning gay marriage, even pondering an amendment to the US Constitution to make it permanent.

Of course, this worked like a charm and Bush won the closest presidential election in US history in a court battle over votes in conservative Florida.

You might recall that after the 2000 election the GOP had a large majority in all 3 branches of government for 8 years. Did gay marriage become illegal in Federal law or in our Constitution? No. Why not?

Well, if you were a Republican lawmaker, why use up and waste an election battle, social issue that could be recycled in some future election to turn out those Christian voters again and again? Indeed. You are being lied to, manipulated, and used to make the wealthy and corporations ever more wealthy. That wealth comes right out of your wallet!

Let's address what some of you are thinking now. You may be thinking, yes but Democratic politicians lie too. This is invariably true. I will argue however, that the scope and impact of their failure to follow through on campaign promises to their voters pales in comparison to the GOP. Example: President Obama made hundreds of campaign promises, and halfway through his term has completed or is working on a significant proportion of them.

Current Status Obama Campaign Promises

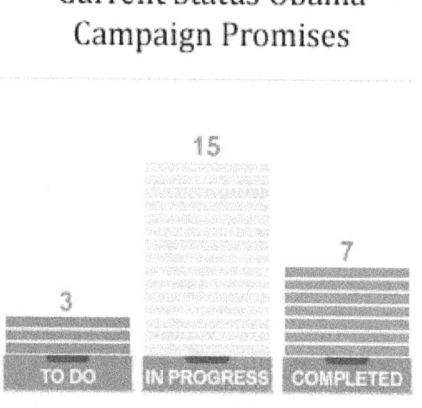

Washington Post, March 2010

According to PolitiFact[19], a fact-checking website, President Obama has fulfilled a large percentage of his promises and is making progress toward many others, and this only halfway through his term. One current news item is President Obama's 2007 campaign promise to join the picket line and protest with Union workers if their rights were being infringed, as they are in the current Union fight in Wisconsin with GOP Governor Scott Walker. Obama has not joined the picket line in Wisconsin. The reasons are clear. Obama hopes to be re-elected. The US voter base is rather evenly split, one-third left, one-third right, and one-third independent (of late independents are as much as 40% of the electorate). Independent voters decide elections, particularly national elections, and Obama is now working to gain the votes of the deciding independent voters, who might cringe at a President walking a protest line.

Still, it is inevitably true that Democrats fail their constituents as well. However, the scope and impact of these failures does not compare to the failure of GOP candidates and the direct negative financial impact on the middle-class in favor of the rich. There are several reasons this is the case. First, Democrats fight for the middle-class, for fair wages, for lower middle-class taxes, for union rights of middle-class working people. They stand for social justice and equality.

With that sort of forum, Democrats simply have no compelling need for grand national strategies like the Southern "Black" Strategy, or the newer Southern "Christian" Strategy to compel voters. Indeed, Democrats are often criticized, even self-criticized for their failure in organizing and strategizing to match the GOP.

Given that Democrat policies and financial philosophies support the middle-class, they can count on large numbers of voters to mobilize in support without an elaborate strategy that is ultimately a lie. The GOP cannot count on such easy support. Certainly big business and wealthy individuals will vote their pocketbooks and therefore vote Republican, but they are a significant minority compared to the large middle-class. As hard as it is for conservative politicians to publicly admit, their war on the middle-class wallet means they must have grand strategies to manipulate independent voters with long unkept campaign promises to win their votes - and villainize the left in the process. Southern Christian voters are their current target, being manipulated by lies that then allow GOP lawmakers to fleece the middle-class and enrich the wealthy.

It is because of these dynamics and for the reasons I have stated, that the argument that Democrats lie and manipulate as much as the GOP is provably false.

Further, the negative impacts of GOP lies to middle-class voters is orders of magnitude higher than the any negative impact of Democratic candidates broken campaign promises.

I have watched politics for many years, noted over and over the disingenuous policies of the GOP, and seen the piling up negative impacts on the middle-class.

Just look at the numbers on incomes for the middle-class and the staggering and growing wealth of the rich - the numbers don't lie. I have also researched and detailed with facts in this writing this same impact. If you care to argue that I am wrong, I would be happy to read your analysis to the contrary. I do not believe it will be an easy, fact-based argument to make.

No, the GOP is alone in the depth, breadth, and negative impact on the nations' economy of their manipulative campaigns to win over Christian voters like you.

Believing these lying politicians is your choice, and I think that is becoming more difficult with each election. Showing Christian voters the truth may be all that stands between the long term success of our economy, the critical middle-class in sustaining our free market economy, and the almost certain demise of America as a great world power.

Sounds ominous, but it is becoming more and more possible that our economy depends on this information awakening on the Christian political right.

The GOP: Hiding within Complexity

The McCain-Feingold Act, Citizens United, and the Union fight in Wisconsin.

These three distinct events in recent US politics are deeply interrelated, although most Americans couldn't say how. Let me talk briefly about each one, then weave together the strategic coherence of all three, as they are intimately interconnected and serve to illustrate the title of this chapter, hiding within complexity. But before I do that, let's talk about why this is important. As we have established, the GOP campaigns to the Christian Right with promises to support social agendas; things like the fight against gay marriage, outlawing abortion rights, disallowing gays in the military, allowing the Ten Commandments to be displayed in Federal Courts, etc. Once elected however, these social issues of the Christian Right never get resolved. Indeed, they are almost never even discussed by the candidate once they gain their office post-election. Instead, the GOP lawmakers work much more aggressively to press their economic agenda. As we have discussed already, this economic agenda is heavily biased toward the wealthy and corporations, and against middle-class America. So how do they get away with that? They hide within complexity, hoping you won't notice what they're really doing to take your money.

As I've mentioned, we are all too busy living our lives; working, raising our children, etc. to pay close attention to the very complex subjects that our lawmakers work on. This complexity allows them to hide, in plain sight, and work against the interests of the middle-class, the very people who elected them. What follows is an example, with a clear desired outcome that helps the wealthy and corporations, and could potentially badly hurt the middle-class for a generation, as we shall see.

In late 2002, Senator John McCain, at the time a moderate Republican in the US Senate, joined forces with a Progressive Democratic Senator Russ Feingold to write the "Bi-Partisan Campaign Reform Act", which is also known as the McCain-Feingold Act. It is just like it sounds, Republican and Democratic Senators got together, created and passed a law that controlled and made transparent, the amount of private money that could come into elections. As is easy to understand, too much hidden money in large quantities in elections tends to compromise the integrity of elected officials. Lobbyists who raise and give this money tend to get their interests met once a politician is elected, and not always in a way that serves the common good. As a matter of fact, it usually harms the middle-class.

A bit more that's important about the McCain-Feingold Act, according to Wikipedia:

"...the McCain-Feingold Act prohibited corporations and unions from using their general treasury funds to make "electioneering communications" or "independent expenditures" (which is defined as "speech that expressly advocates the election or defeat of a candidate and that is made independently of a candidate's campaign")."

The act became law in early 2003. So that's McCain-Feingold. So, let's then move to Citizens United, then how the two are related.

One year later, during the 2004 presidential campaign, again according to Wikipedia:

"Citizens United, a conservative nonprofit organization, filed a complaint before the Federal Election Commission charging that ads for Michael Moore's film Fahrenheit 9/11, which was highly critical of the Bush administration's response to the terrorist attacks on September 11, 2001, constituted political advertising and as such violated election law and could not be aired 60 days before an election or 30 days before a party convention."

The Federal Election Committee (FEC) dismissed a further complaint filed in 2005, holding that the commission could find no reason to believe the respondents violated the Act because the film, associated trailers and website represented bona fide commercial activity, not "contributions" or "expenditures" as defined by the Federal Election Campaign Act.

Flash-forward to the 2008 election.

In the presidential primaries, Hillary Clinton, then a Senator from New York was the presumptive front-runner against a less well-known Senator from Illinois, Barack Obama. Hillary was the most obvious threat to a GOP presidential election victory, and the Republican establishment was keen to attack her stance on a broad range of issues and positions. Given the outcome of the Michael Moore Film Fahrenheit 9/11, and the potential power that film had in swaying public opinion against George W. Bush, the GOP adopted this strategy which served as a blue-print for Republicans to attack Clinton in the form of an unflattering film about her positions – which they found were against their own views and would fire up the Republican base.

According to Wikipedia again:

"In the wake of the ruling on Michael Moore's film Fahrenheit 9/11, [the decisions that allowed the promotion of the documentary Fahrenheit 9/11 during the 2004 campaign], Citizens United (again, a conservative non-profit) sought to run television commercials during the 2008 campaign promoting its political documentary Hillary: The Movie, which was critical of then-Senator Hillary Clinton, and to air the movie on DirecTV.

In January 2008, the United States District Court for the District of Columbia ruled that the commercials violated provisions in the Bipartisan Campaign Reform Act of 2002 (McCain-Feingold) restricting "electioneering communications" 30 days before primaries.

Though the political action committee claimed that their film was fact-based and nonpartisan, the lower Court found that the film had no purpose other than to discredit Clinton's candidacy for President and it was not allowed to air."

This uneven outcome in similar cases; Fahrenheit 9/11 criticizing Bush being allowed to air before the 2004 election, and Hillary: The Movie, criticizing

Clinton NOT being allowed to air before the 2008 election; led to a Supreme Court challenge of McCain-Feingold on grounds of Free Speech.

The Supreme Court in a 5-4 ruling (5 GOP appointed Justices, vs. 4 Democratic appointed Justices, right down party lines) struck down a provision of the McCain-Feingold Act that prohibited all corporations, both for-profit and not-for-profit, and unions from broadcasting "electioneering communications." This essentially undid McCain-Feingold, and meant that two groups, corporations and unions were now allowed by the Supreme Court of the United States to spend unlimited dollars from their general treasury funds to make "electioneering communications" or "independent expenditures".

What resulted in the 2010 elections was staggering. Funding that normally flowed to the Republican National Committee, now flowed to newly-formed non-profit GOP-supporting organizations from large corporation, and dues collecting business advocates like the US Chamber of Commerce. These non-profits raised millions of dollars, and ran their own Democratic attack ads in the thousands in states where Republicans were behind.

Indeed, the 5-4 decision of the right-dominated Supreme Court changed forever the face of US elections, favoring two groups - corporations on the Right and unions on the Left - to spend in an unlimited fashion and to curry favor with and influence lawmakers. Seems at least equitable so far right?

Wrong.

Corporations have many times more money than labor unions, and clearly prefer Republicans with their business-friendly, middle-class harming policies that shift power and income to corporations and away from the middle-class.

Now, the last part of this complex story.

Union busting.

According to Wikipedia:

"The 2011 Wisconsin protests are a series of on-going demonstrations in the United States involving tens of thousands of protesters including union members, students, and other citizens.

The protests began on February 15, 2011 in opposition to certain provisions in legislation proposed by Republican Governor of Wisconsin Scott Walker to address a projected $3.6 billion budget shortfall.

The legislation would require state employees to contribute 5.8% of their salaries to cover pension costs, contribute 12.6% towards their health care premiums, and would weaken collective bargaining rights for most public employee union members. Democrats and union leaders offered to accept the increased cost of benefits but not the removal of bargaining rights. Walker rejected the idea."

At the time of this writing in early March 2011, the stand-off is still underway, and whether the union will be busted is still undecided.

So why would Governor Walker reject the union offer?

He is trying to solve a budget crisis and the unions agreed to all his financial requests for increased union contributions on pensions and health care premiums. They simply want to retain the right to band together and negotiate - called "Collective Bargaining", a right they have had for 50 years in Wisconsin.

Why would the governor stand firm and reject their idea? After all, what could agreeing to sit down and negotiate (collectively bargain) have to do with a budget crisis.

The sad truth is collective bargaining has nothing to do with the budget crisis - despite lies from the GOP lawmakers in Wisconsin and in the US Federal government.

So what is going on?

Remember the Supreme Court ruling in Citizens United that allowed unions and corporations to spend unlimited funds in elections? In the 2010 election, you can look at the top 10 contributors to all campaigns, both Republican and Democrat. Seven of the top 10 are non-profits raising money for Republicans from corporations and a handful of wealthy right-leaning individuals. The other 3 in the top 10?

You guessed it. Unions.

If the GOP can destroy collective bargaining, starting in Wisconsin - the birthplace of US Unions, why would working people join unions in the first place? They wouldn't. There would simply be no reason for union workers to pay unions dues. Union incomes would plummet, and in the 2012 elections, ALL of the top 10 contributors to the election will be corporations and wealthy individuals - all funding a GOP win.

That's how The McCain-Feingold Act, is connected to Citizens

United, which is connected to the Union fight in Wisconsin and spreading to other states with GOP Governors. Ohio GOP Governor John Kasich has already outlawed collective bargaining in Ohio, by executive decree. And more GOP states are pondering this same kind of move.

As you can see, the intense complexity of the above multi-part story means most Americans will not see this interrelatedness and because they don't see it, they won't see the truth of what the GOP is really up to. It's a complex and confusing story to most people; people very busy working and raising their children, and a story too complicated to bother paying attention. But it represents a theme. It is the most important action the GOP is taking to gain even more power. And remember, once in power they do not help the middle-class, or even vote for Christian social issue like abortion or gay marriage. No, they press their economic agenda to keep middle-class people from becoming richer, and making the rich and corporations even more wealthy.

The mask of this complexity is an opportunity for the GOP as well, to convince their Christian conservative social issue voters that the GOP "means business" and is aggressively trying to end abortion and to stop gay marriage, and other right-wing social agendas. So what do they do? GOP politicians, since being sworn into office in January 2010, just 3 months in office at the time of this writing, have passed lots of "Christian social issue" inspired laws in the GOP-controlled US House, the only branch of government where the GOP currently has a majority.

You can't be surprised, given this new perspective on what they're up to, that since taking office in January 2011, the GOP lawmakers there have passed no less than four bills seeking to weaken abortion laws nationally. You also can no longer fail to notice, that these GOP lawmakers are not really serious about making these bills into laws against abortion rights. They are safe, in the GOP-led US House, to pass as many bills like this as they like - no one can stop them from passing bills, they're in the majority in the US House. But this is not a serious effort to stop abortion - as the GOP lawmakers know the bills will never become law. The Democratically controlled Senate and White House will never sign them into law. These GOP House members are simply passing these abortion-limiting laws to convince you, their Christian middle-class voter base that they are "listening to you". They're not. They're just playing to the crowd, yet another step in their deception.

So the GOP House gets to make headlines in their "gallant fight to listen to Christian voters and stop abortions". While the complex connections of McCain-Feingold, Citizens United, and Union-busting in Wisconsin are too complex for most voters to follow. As such, middle-class voters don't see the complex story as what it is; the GOP power-grab to continue their economic agenda in favor of the rich.

These GOP House members are sure you'll see the House passing abortion-limiting legislation. I'd bet they're right, as I would bet you've heard about these abortion-limiting bills. Surely that is the case, and most Christian Conservatives have surely read, with excitement, about the multiple bills the US House passed in only 3 months to limit abortion - and felt very well represented in Washington. If that's how you feel, you are being fooled, and if you fall for this, you are part of the problem. Essentially, by continuing to believe these lies of the GOP, by voting for them, you're stealing money from yourself. Crazy, but true.

Of course, what really matters to these GOP politicians is NOT abortion. Indeed, many of these abortion bills simply reiterate what is already in existing laws - for instance that Federal funds cannot be used for abortion. Why pass a bill that is already law? Right, to remind you they're listening to you. Please.

It is this complex set of issues surrounding trying to kill

unions to win future elections for the GOP that is what GOP lawmakers really care about, not abortion limits or any other Christian social issues. These lawmakers know that killing unions will allow the GOP the power to more successfully implement their rich-people-favoring and corporation-favoring financial agenda; make rich people and corporations richer.

They want more power to give money to the wealthy, after all rich people and corporations must be paid back for their large, anonymous donations now that those are legal after the Supreme Court's 'Citizens United' case - and in making the rich and corporations more wealthy, they will once again fleece the bank accounts of their GOP middle-class voters.

I hope you can see that our GOP politicians hide within the complexity of our government, acting as if they are supporting your social agenda, but all the while taking money from your pocket and giving it to corporations and the wealthy.

In any other context, this would be called manipulation and theft.

The Tea Party, a grassroots effort? Hardly

If you're a fiscal conservative by nature, you are likely excited by the grassroots movement that sprang up in 2009 and called itself "The Tea Party". This is a loosely knit set of groups with somewhat different goals, but a general theme of smaller government, lower taxes, and fiscal efforts to force the Federal government to balance budgets, reduce debt, and live within its' means. All good so far, right?

But there is ample proof that the Tea Party is largely not an organic phenomenon, born out of voter frustration. It is not largely a grassroots organization that simply sprang up to accomplish the above things. Let's lay out some facts you may not be aware of about this "grassroots" effort.

Business interests care deeply about getting GOP candidates elected, as once in office, GOP candidates support economic policies slanted toward business and the wealthy. Indeed almost all GOP candidates and lawmakers share an over-riding economic philosophy that what drives the economy is business, and middle-class consumers are much less important - or at least of subordinate importance to business. In this "supply side" economic view, the levers of government are best focused on bestowing economic power via low taxation toward business, not the middle-class.

The theory being that low taxes on business creates the right economic certainty for businesses to risk expansion, investing, and creating ever more jobs - an outcome that is good for the overall economy. In this philosophical construct, consumers are assumed to be indirectly benefited, as business expansion means more jobs. More jobs leads to more competition for top talent, and wages will inevitably rise chasing scarce industry talent. You'll often hear supply side fans arguing that government can't create jobs; only the free market can create jobs. For the most part this is true. Government can largely only create the conditions to create jobs, but the bulk of jobs must be created by supply and demand in the free market. What supply side aficionados often forget is that free markets have two sides, supply (business) and demand (consumers), and without a healthy environment for both, free markets cannot flourish.

In some sense, supply side economics is a logical philosophy - and during certain times in our history has been critical to growth. We are no longer in that part of history and the endless assault on middle-class consumers by this "false summit" of GOP supply-side economic theory must be not only moderated, but reversed. It can't be continued and accelerated, as is the desire of the GOP. Supply-side economics had a time when it worked. The GOP would like you as a middle-class consumer, to think it is endlessly a good thing. History however, shows a very different outcome.

While in our history good things have indeed transpired from low taxation on business, and innovation leading to economic growth can and do occur, supply-side economics is not an exclusive panacea for driving the economy ever forward. The supply and demand sides of the free market engine must remain healthy. As we have shown, the demand side has been suffering for most of our lives.

David Cay Johnston, Pulitzer-winning *New York Times* reporter and economist, discusses this bias toward the supply side, and not the demand side as follows:

Demand Side[20] [the name of Johnston's blog] sees an inverse relationship between tax cuts for the rich and efficient economic activity. These big bonuses to those most self-interested means the masters of capitalism (aka the slaves of greed) are leading the economy. Hardly what you want for broad-based, stable and sustainable growth."

In his excellent book, entitled *"Free Lunch: How The Wealthiest Americans Enrich Themselves At Government Expense (and Stick you With the Bill)*[21], Johnston coherently argues that the middle-class are being duped, sending the wealth from the middle-class to the wealthy. He goes on:

"[In 1979 during his run to the White House] Ronald Reagan famously asked Americans if we were better off than we were four year ago; Americans said "no" and elected him. This empowered a great change, supposedly, in government. It was supposed to lead to less government, more market solutions, and lower taxes. What I'm asking in *Free Lunch* is: 'Are you better off than you were a generation ago when Reagan was elected?' Government is just as big, there are vastly more regulations, and as I show, we have many new rules and regulations that handcuff the invisible hand of the market and instead, in subtle, sometimes hidden, ways, extract money from the pockets of the many [the middle-class] and funnel it to the politically connected few [the wealthy and corporations]. It's the very thing that Adam Smith[22] [broadly considered the father of free market economic theory] said would ruin the benefits of markets."

So if you think that Republican economic philosophy helps protect the US free market, you would struggle to prove that, especially in the last 30 years.

Republican economic philosophy is destroying the power of our free market, by over-favoring the supply-side of the equation.

Again, they do this out of either a misunderstanding of the negative impact of their ideas, or in some cases, purposefully ignore the harm to serve their own, selfish careers and reward their wealthy corporate and rich campaign financiers.

Remember, GOP candidates simply must have the backing of the wealthy, corporations, and dupe the middle-class (using social issues of southern racism, and more recently Christian middle-class voters) to stay in office.

So how does all of this relate to the Tea Party movement?

The Tea Party movement is, once again, largely an elaborate ruse, couched in the terms of fiscal sanity and lower taxes, to fool middle-class voters into coming to the polls to elect or re-elect Republicans. It is disingenuous and a ruse because it is anything but grassroots. The Tea Party may have begun as a grassroots effort, but it was quickly co-opted by wealthy conservative activists. It was fully funded, conceived, organized, and launched by two powerful billionaire businessmen[23]

In an excellent exposé, NY Times columnist Frank Rich[24] outlines the fact that the Tea Party was conceived, funded, organized, and encouraged by the billionaire Koch brothers.

An excerpt from the article:

"Tea Partiers may share the Koch's' detestation of taxes, big government and Obama. But there's a difference between mainstream conservatism and a fringe agenda [of the Koch brothers] that tilts completely toward big business, whether on Wall Street or in the Gulf of Mexico, while dismantling fundamental government safety nets designed to protect the unemployed, public health, workplace safety and the subsistence of the elderly [also known as, the middle class]."

The Koch brother's clearly see the benefit of electing more Republicans to the US government, as they know these lawmakers will favor business and the wealthy - at the expense of the middle-class.

It is a safe, cost-benefit to them to spend millions to spur on the Tea Party, encouraging middle-class Americans to think it's good for them, knowing that the movement's success will elect more Republicans, who will not favor the Tea Party faithful middle-class, who are largely Christian middle-class voters, but only favor business and the wealthy.

Remember the connections we explored between campaign finance and the benefit to the GOP of destroying Unions in Chapter 3?

Average Americans might miss the connection between helping get Republicans elected and destroying Union collective bargaining rights, but the Koch brothers clearly see this insidious connection. The Daily Kos, a democratic-leaning blog created by Markos Moulitsas, writes the following:

"Oh my, we got ourselves quite a tail-wagging going on in Wisconsin. You are thinking, what? This is about collective bargaining and workers' rights! Bullshit. You are being wagged. As always this has to do with money, and the union "compromise" coming down the pipe was set up to be the "booby" prize while the Koch Brothers get their "booty" prize. This is all being well-orchestrated with an end game that has absolutely nothing to do with unions. As I said in comments before, to much bewilderment, this is about power plants and a vertical monopoly the Koch Brothers have their eye on in Wisconsin."

Once again, Christian voters and other Tea Party supporting middle-class Americans are being duped. Used to drive more Republicans into office where, as we have shown over and over, will favor business and the wealthy - at the direct expense of the solvency and stability of you - middle-class, largely Christian American voters.

Wake up, Christians and other middle class Americans. You are being used, stoked by social issues to get you to vote for the GOP, who turn around and harm you, directly.

You have a direct hand in your own self-destruction.

The Christian Turing Test

There is currently a fascinating book on the market entitled, "The Most Human Human"[25] written by Brian Christian. He is participating in an annual competition wherein participants, made up of several humans and several computers, interact over text chat with a panel of judges. The judges don't know if the conversation they're having over text chat is with another human, or a computer. The judges have to decide, after a 5 minute chat, if the conversation they just had was with a human or a computer. This kind of test has been around for a long time. It's called a Turing test, invented by English mathematician and computer scientist Alan Turing.

At the end of the computer/human Turing Test contest, the judges determine if any of the competing computers could indeed fool the panel that the computer was a human being. They award a prize to the team who built the successful computer software that fooled at least 30% of the judges. They also award a prize for the most human, human - that hidden person who most convinced the judges they were indeed *not* a computer. It's a fascinating concept and contest. The computers are getting close to making it impossible for the judges to root them out as computers feigning to be humans.

But the prize for the most human, human. That sounds like an election, where we pick the most presidential, President.

This began me thinking about the Turing test in a political context. Our politician's campaign on ideas, philosophies, and concepts, working to convince us that they're vision for leading is something we are for or against. They do this with a dizzying array of strategies; appealing to the middle (left-leaning Republicans, or right-leaning Democrats, the largest swing voters in any election), stirring (or pandering to be pejorative), to their base. For Democrats this means pushing social justice buttons and an aversion to the casual use of US military power. For Republicans this invariably is pontificating on God, family, morality - the "dog whistles" of the ideological right. Politicians of both parties do this with varying levels of success. But worse, it's clear that some politicians do this disingenuously. It's usually easy to see, but not always.

You've seen Democratic candidates with generally moderate, centrist views talking about social justice in ways that seem inauthentic. Alternately, you see Republican candidates with a past of dubious distinction (criminal activities, moral failings, and questionable religiosity) speaking as if they are Jesus Christ himself. My own personal view is: a) this is to be expected in competitive political races and as such not necessarily a bad thing, but more troubling b) is dangerous and manipulative.

Let's pick a yardstick of negative potential impact from false-pandering. We could pick many, but for our purposes, let's focus on the negative potential impact of false-pandering and the accompanying negative impact on free market economies. Democratic false-pandering (stirring the left-leaning base disingenuously) leads to disappointment on the progress of society for those in the liberal left who wish for the advancement of civil liberties for all, firm but fair social safety nets, etc. It is in my view that this pandering is much less insidious than the false-pandering on the right - at least in the past 30 years. Let me explain further.

If a Democrat actually succeeds in implementing left-leaning ideology, we get universal health care, Social Security, Medicare, less military intervention. If a Republican actually succeeds in implementing right-leaning ideology, we get corporate welfare, wealthy rich people, middle-class decay, and more military intervention. The latter seems more dangerous by almost any measure.

Watch political news almost any day and you will see this kind of pandering, in my view mostly false-pandering. I've just watched the first political speeches for the upcoming 2012 election. Five Republican Presidential hopefuls in conservative Iowa[26] (an early primary state) discussing their views on America and our governmental policies.

Now remember, these speeches are in the context of a country founded on the principles of secular, self-governing, a-religious philosophies laid out by our founding documents. So what was the overwhelming theme of these GOP hopeful speeches?

Jobs? After all, we're in a deep recession and millions of Americans are out of work

Finance? After all, lots of people - and for good reason - are concerned about government spending and deficits

Education? After all, American schools are routinely rated as poor and falling farther behind the rest of the world

Health care? After all, 30 million Americans are uninsured, many children, and our President's controversial health care act stirs lots of passion on both sides

No, these issues barely even came up.

The vast majority of the content of every speech was, of course, God and the candidates' views on morality in public policy and how Democrats are leading our country into moral decay. Please.

This from an array of politicians, almost all with highly suspect pasts in the arena of traditional Judeo-Christian values. As an example, there are many, Newt Gingrich has been married 3 times, was proven to have misappropriated House funds while Speaker, and was publicly reprimanded by the House at large. Gingrich eventually resigned his Speakership under a cloud of ethical controversy. It is even now known that while railing against then President Clinton for his moral failings in the Monica Lewinsky scandal, Gingrich himself was involved in a sexual affair while married. Gingrich is hardly a bastion of conservative values. As comedian Steven Colbert quipped,

"If elected, Gingrich would not have a first lady; he'd have a third lady."

Funny, but seriously is a thrice married President someone who displays the Judeo-Christian "family" values so important to conservative Christians? I think not.

Still, he and the other 4 GOP hopefuls pontificated with great passion, anger, and defiance on the importance of God, faith, morality, as if they were the Pope himself.

Why do they do this? Because it's what you, as a Christian Conservative want to hear.

Even if they don't believe it, and don't care - they want your vote and this is a proven way to ensure it.

It's like they're playing an elaborate Christian Turing Test. If they can convince you they are a bona fide believer, a true Christian, you will vote for them no matter what else they believe. Surely these values in a President, particularly if they are feigned (as they almost always are), are not more important to you than your own families prosperity? You know that GOP candidates, whether they are really bona fide Christians or not, once in office will simply ignore the social issues important to you, and implement fiscal policies which will enrich the wealthy at your expense.

Watch these candidates with this in mind and I think you might start to be troubled by not only their willingness to do this, but your own very real culpability in insisting that the Christian Turing test (false-pontification on Christian social issues) more important than your own financial prosperity, and the future prosperity of your children and grand children.

Listen differently and judge for yourself, but more importantly think about what matters most to you, and vote with that in mind. What's the old saying, "You better watch out for yourself, because no one else will."

The GOP strategy of (Pseudo) Crisis Leverage

As we have seen in previous chapters, the GOP has an inherent numbers disadvantage in elections, given that there are vastly more middle-class voters than wealthy individuals with a primary interest in big business. An honest assessment of the economic policy actions - not their positions, which are often feigned as we have discussed - but looking at GOP economic policy actions alone reveals little in the way of attractiveness to the middle-class. Tax breaks, always a GOP favorite, almost never accrue to the middle-class where they will have the most economically stimulative effect, but are always pushed by the GOP to the wealthy and big business.

As we have shown, this numbers disadvantage problem means the GOP has little choice but to exaggerate their fondness for social and cultural weaknesses among the electorate as a means of enfranchising those so inclined to vote Republican, even against their own middle-class best interests. The GOP has been stunningly successful with this approach for the last 30 years - leveraging racist anger in white Southern voters to turn the reliably Democratic South into a GOP stronghold.

When racism began to fade as a useful tool to fan the racist flames of Southern white anger to move them toward the GOP, conservative strategists revised this disingenuous "Southern Strategy" to now target the soft spots in social unrest among conservative Christians; touting their piety for issues such as making gay marriage illegal, fighting abortion rights, ever more unimpeded access to guns, and generally championing the desire from Christian conservatives to push Judeo-Christian morality into our government, despite the clear separation of Church and State outlined by our Constitution.

An example of the last item is George W. Bush's "Faith-based Initiative" which skirts, barely, the separation of church and state by funneling millions of dollars in taxpayer money to religious organizations - who are tax-exempt and can spend the money in any way they see fit, including helping to fund GOP local and national election pushes. This and other quasi-legal actions are lauded by conservative Christians, and seem to excite their fervor for their religion. This further enfranchises them to become loyal GOP voters - despite the economic harm the GOP regularly shovels onto them all the while.

But there are other strategies at play in the GOP to overcome the endemic problems that their big-business, wealthy-American favoring policies would otherwise undermine. Chief among these alternative strategies is something I like to call, "(Pseudo) Crisis Leverage".

The word, "Pseudo" is in parenthesis because sometimes the GOP makes up the crisis, and other times they use a very real crisis to accomplish things that, while not solving the crisis, do provide cover for their real aims.

"(Pseudo) Crisis Leverage" is where a crisis is used, or even an invented crisis is leveraged to provide cover for middle-class harming policy.

Prime examples are numerous and abundant; we'll explore two of the more recent of these "crisis leveraging" moves by the disingenuous GOP Governors in Michigan and Florida - or if you will, the "Two Lying Ricks".

Michigan GOP Governor Rick Snyder and the budget crisis as opportunity to redistribute wealth to business

First, let's focus on state efforts by GOP Governors to use the "pseudo-crisis leverage" strategy as a mask to give big business and the wealthy ever more of our money. In Michigan, GOP governor Rick Snyder has taken a very real budget shortfall there (at least it's a real crisis in this case), and used that budget crisis to increase taxes. That seems reasonable right?

Well, guess who the tax hike is applied to in Michigan? According to the Associated Press[27], the tax is applied only to,

"Low-income wage earners, senior citizens, and those who make donations to schools".

Well, that seems pretty unfair doesn't it? Why not tax everyone including businesses and the wealthy. Could it be perhaps that Michigan businesses and wealthy citizens support and donate to Governor Snyder's elections campaign? Right, they do.

Still, a tax hike seems reasonable to fix a budget crisis - so does this tax hike address the budget crisis in Michigan? Of course not. The governor also has announced a massive tax cut for businesses in Michigan.

A $1.7B tax HIKE on low-income workers, the elderly, and those giving donations to schools

And, a $1.8B tax BREAK to businesses in Michigan

It's straightforward math. The governor's plan actually makes the Michigan budget $100M worse! So when the governor claims "This tax hike is about the budget", that is a hard argument to make without a large dose of chutzpah, spin, and downright dishonesty. This is a classic case that illustrates the GOP strategy of using a crisis (real or imagined) to redistribute wealth from the poor and the middle-class, to the wealthy and to business.

Of course, the Michigan governor makes all the right noises about his Christian values. Governor Snyder in his campaign materials has the following policy positions. He is, and I quote:

- Firmly pro-life, which begins at conception
- Embryos are human life
- Opposes federal abortion funding

- Absolutely uphold the 2nd Amendment
- Opposes restrictions on the right to bear arms
- Opposes government run health care
- Opposes affirmative action

Clearly the dog-whistle positions of Christian conservatives are tooting.

Is the fact that he stands for the things above, which are already law, already protected, and not at risk - is that enough to justify him taking your money and giving it to business? I think not.

Florida GOP Governor Rick Scott and the budget crisis as opportunity to redistribute wealth to business

In Florida, newly elected GOP Governor Rick Scott is executing the same play from the GOP "pseudo crisis leverage" playbook. Florida has a very real budget crisis. So of course, according to the Palm Beach Post[28], Gov. Scott has proposed a massive funding cut of $1.75B in education funding. Seems like a bad place to reduce funding, but there is a very real crisis, so that's reasonable right?

Except, as in Michigan, Florida Gov. Scott is also proposing a $1.6B Tax CUT for Florida businesses. Again, just as in Michigan, this cut in school funding is disingenuously couched as an effort to address a very real budget problem in Florida, but those are just words. The actions of Rick Scott are completely undermining that logic, as the money is simply transferred from schools and middle-class children, to business interests.

Again I ask, is the Florida governors' stance on GOP-favorite social issues enough for middle-class GOP voters that they are willing to have their children's school funding slashed, simply to give corporations in Florida a massive infusion of cash?

It does not follow logically that this could be true. As widely reported in media across the political spectrum, America's businesses have used the recent recession to cut back on everything from wages to benefits, and are currently sitting on massive amounts of un-invested cash. According to the Washington Independent Newspaper[29],

"Non-financial companies are sitting on $1.8 trillion in cash, roughly one-quarter more than at the beginning of the recession. And as several major firms report impressive earnings this week, the money continues to flow into firms' coffers."

So why exactly does Governor Scott think this is a critical transfer of wealth to business?

To what end? Is it just a payback for supporting his recent election? Surely not, but what else could it be?

Did either of these Governors campaign on this approach? Of course not. What would they say? I am going to gut school funding and give the money to big business.

Or I am going to tax the poor and the elderly and give the money to business.

Ridiculous, right? But that is exactly what they do once in office. If you are middle-class and voted for these Governors, you have just cut your own throat - again.

Troubling questions with no clear answer but continues to nag at this question: What are Christian conservative voters doing in supporting the GOP that serves their own needs? It seems, frankly that none of the middle-class Christian conservatives own best interests are served with this GOP support - a shocking conclusion, but verifiably valid and difficult to assess in any other way.

It would seem that the satisfaction that Christian social issue drums are being beat is enough for GOP voters, even though almost no legislation ever moves backward in the more conservative direction and toward the hopes of these Christian conservatives. It seems touting Christian conservative values (while doing nothing to legislate accordingly) is enough for you, even when it means these same GOP candidates turn around and take your money, only to give it to the wealthy and to corporations.

Once again, another in a piling up of strikes against the middle-class from GOP lawmakers, and no progress at all on Christian conservative issues. Is that really what you voted for? I doubt it. But that is indeed what you've done to yourself and your middle-class Christian neighbors.

It's truly insanity.

Why the GOP must seek power at the expense
of US middle-class economic health

The dogged determination of the GOP to organize around their strategic options is impressive. Perhaps it is because of the numbers problem they have in elections given that there are vastly more middle-class voters than wealthy individuals with a primary interest in big business.

Or perhaps it is something more endemic to conservatives in general, a predisposition if you will, to organizing around a single set of core beliefs. We'll examine the conservative mindset and its relationship to faith in the next chapter.

Let's turn our attention to a troubling trend among conservative lawmakers to seek power, even at the expense of our economy. Since the GOP victory in the 2010 elections, where the GOP took majority control over the US House of Representatives, much has been made in the press about the way they govern in the House.

The main lever of control in the House is appropriations, the setting of budgets for the US government. Economists largely agree that jobs in the US economy are almost exclusively created by the private sector, and not by government. Economists further largely agree that government's main role in stimulating job growth is to implement laws and policies that set the stage for private sector job growth.

To do this, government can reduce business taxes, can offer tax credits for certain types of private sector growth, but the main factor that stimulates business growth is consumer demand. Demand from consumers seeking to purchase goods and services.

Without this demand, businesses find investments in supply creation are simply too risky. So another important lever the US government has to stimulate growth is to put more money in the hands of consumers. In general, this demand-side strategy is not favored by the GOP. In fact it is despised.

It's an odd omission to GOP fiscal strategies that they largely ignore the demand-side (consumers) in favor of the supply-side (business), as the simple logic of stimulating the consumer demand seems such an obvious positive stimulant to the economy.

Economists, particularly those who believe in Keynesian-style government investment, realize that both the demand and supply side of the market are important. Indeed, in a down economy, the most stimulative approach the government can take would be to get more money into the hands of consumers.

Tax cuts for the wealthy, as we have shown, have only limited effect, and tax breaks for business only set the stage for business expansion. Without consumer demand, businesses will not invest and expand, as businesses wait for the demand to increase - reducing their risk. Given this, it is odd, if not intentionally obstructive for GOP lawmakers to favor business interests at the expense of consumer interests.

Remember, businesses are sitting on large amounts of un-invested cash - waiting for demand to increase. Giving them more money in the form of tax breaks just adds to their unspent coffers. So why not stimulate demand by lowering taxes on consumers, getting cash into their hands, stimulating demand, and thereby encourage business to invest the money they're sitting on in their balance sheets?

One could easily conclude from the set of economic circumstances listed above - all verifiably true - that the US government would be focused on spending (or tax cuts) to stimulate consumer demand. The GOP is NOT focused on this, not at all.

Since being elected to take control of the House, and it's power to appropriate, the GOP lawmakers there have not passed a single piece of legislation to stimulate consumer demand. Indeed, they are hyper-focused on the complete opposite - cutting spending.

The recent GOP-led House proposal to cut between $60B and $100B from the current year budget has been almost unanimously characterized by economists of all stripes, as causing further contraction of the US economy - and will result in further job loss. Ben Bernanke, appointed Federal Reserve chairman by George W. Bush and served on Bush's Council of Economic Advisers has discussed this with Congress. Bernanke is a conservative by nature, but he points out the following about the GOP-led House proposal to cut spending.

Federal Reserve Chairman Ben Bernanke said Wednesday a Republican spending cut plan would not cause a big dent to U.S. economic growth, but could cost around 200,000 jobs over two years[30].

Bernanke said that a $60 billion cut along the lines being pursued by Republicans in the House would likely trim growth by around two-tenths of a percentage point in the first year and one-tenth in the next year.

"That would translate into a couple of hundred thousand jobs. So it's not trivial," he said in response to questions from members of the House Financial Services Committee.

Pressed on how such job losses would affect the recovery.

"I would like to see job creation," he said. "What I have been trying to focus on is, we have got to keep our eye on deficit reduction, but we need to think about it in a long-term framework."

The Republican-run House has passed a budget bill for the current fiscal year that includes $61 billion in spending cuts, but majority Democrats in the Senate say the reductions would endanger the economic recovery.

As you may recall, the GOP members who took over the House roundly criticized President Obama during the 2010 election campaign for not focusing enough on jobs.

The GOP campaigned heavily that their primary focus would be jobs. In fact many GOP lawmakers in the House continue to say they are focused on jobs. Majority leader Eric Cantor tweeted this repeatedly of late.

Here's an example:

> Today's jobs report reveals far too many
> people remain out of work; that's why all
> our efforts are centered around jobs
> http://j.mp/eWEFf7
>
> 3 minutes ago via web
> Retweeted by 6 people
>
>  GOPLeader
> Eric Cantor

So are GOP lawmakers like Cantor focused on jobs? The answer is a resounding "no".

Mr. Cantor links to a press release[31] about jobs. He doesn't take you to House Resolution, or H.R. 1[32], a funding bill called "Full-Year Continuing Appropriations Act". Nor does Cantor mention H.R.2[33], the so-called "Repealing the Job-Killing Health Care Law Act" which as you can see has the phrase "Job-Killing" in the title but really seeks to repeal health reform. Nor does Cantor mention H.R. 3[34], the "No Taxpayer Funding for Abortion Act".

Do any of these sound like reasoned efforts by the GOP-led House to stimulate job growth? No. H.R.2 makes vague reference to "job killing" but that is an implication that has only a speculative basis in fact, but H.R.2 does fit nicely into what the GOP likes to believe - businesses need certainty to grow.

Yes. But businesses are more driven by consumer demand. Where is the focus on demand? It does not exist from the GOP.

How could this be? It seems entirely plausible that the GOP cares not at all about increasing job growth while President Obama is in the White House. Why? Because if jobs are created, the President will likely get most of the credit. Conversely, if job growth does not occur, the President will likewise largely be blamed by the electorate - making it more likely that a GOP presidential candidate can unseat him.

Cynical, but what else can explain the fact that the GOP-led House has no interest in stimulating consumer demand, the number one issue most likely to create jobs?

It certainly seems clear that while in the minority, the GOP strategy is to quietly make things worse, to stir voter discontent and frustration, and thereby encourage a protest vote against the incumbents. No GOP lawmaker would ever admit to such a devious strategy, but their actions belie their feigned focus on job creation. Since Democrats are in control of everything in the Federal government except the House, this minority strategy of slowing the country to harm Democrats and Obama in particular, places a higher priority on defeating the Democrats than it does on encouraging the country's economy back to health faster.

Are you willing to remain jobless, or to remain in a poor economy simply to allow discontent to increase the potential of a GOP election win in 2012? No, few could answer that question honestly in the affirmative. It's a terrible thing to place political power over the health of our country, but the GOP seems to care more about power than they do recovery. As a stronger recovery harms their re-election chances in 2012.

So again it begs the questions: Is voting for your Christian social agenda more important than your job, your families' financial health? I doubt it. Are you willing to remain unemployed, underemployed, or under paid - increasing your own personal debt, delaying further your potential retirement date, simply to give Republicans power in our government? It's difficult to imagine anyone voting for that outcome.

Further, when will Christian conservative voters realize that the GOP is too dependent on the conservative hot button social issues to really be interested in addressing them? Doing so would put them back on a level playing field to attract voters - undermine their new "Southern Christian Strategy" discussed earlier, and eventually turn the voter tide toward

Democrats and more consumer-focused Republicans. So voting for your conservative social agenda not only fails to get it addressed, but in the meantime means your job, your savings, your children's college education, your retirement, all are at risk.

Surely this logical view of the sanity of a GOP vote should trouble conservative Christians.

Does it trouble you? It should.

The Conservative Psyche

Faith has often been described as "belief without evidence".

Much of Christian faith is predicated on not only belief without evidence, but strengthens the argument that faith in the face of minimal evidence is even more spiritually meaningful as it represents a test, presumably by God himself, as to the fidelity of the Christian faithful in the face of minimal proof, or even counter-evidence, and calls them to trust in scripture over all rational objections.

To rationalists, this feature of Christian faith is a circular argument, that goes something like this: There is no definitive proof that God even exists much less cares about us, but the bible states that this means God wants you to believe in Him as a test of your faith. Circular arguments are by definition largely irrational, as they tend to be self-fulfilling prophecies, leading one to a predetermined answer, rather than an answer born of rational thought, and therefore leads one to self-deception.

Let's ponder a simpler (and less loaded) circular argument as example. If I told you my body was made of wood, and I'm five hundred years old, and this is written in a book penned by an unseen, unproven, but infallible being, would that make it so simply because I said so?

Of course, not.

According to Wikipedia[35], some rationalists criticize religious faith arguing its irrationality, and see faith as ignorance of reality: a strong belief in something with no evidence and sometimes a strong belief in something even with evidence against it. Bertrand Russell, a British philosopher, logician, mathematician, historian, and social critic noted,

"Where there is evidence, no one speaks of 'faith'. We do not speak of faith that two and two are four or that the earth is round. We only speak of faith when we wish to substitute emotion for evidence."

No matter your views on this, faith; committed belief without evidence, or even when there is mounting counter-evidence, is a key philosophical tenant at the very foundation of those who call themselves Christians.

Ken R. Abell, an author and advocate of lifelong learning, argues that,

"Belief determines mindset—mindset determines behavior. That simple statement has far-reaching ramifications that we seldom comprehend.

We often miss the connection between our belief system and how we conduct our lives." While Abell reaches idealist religious conclusions about how Christians conduct their lives to live their faith, this idea that our belief determines our mindset, and therefore our mindset determines our behavior, provides potentially powerful explanatory postulate and illuminating insights into the voting behavior and philosophical political calculus of Christian conservative voters.

A rationalist would be hard pressed to vote counter to their own personal needs. If a government policy will directly harm them, it is illogical, indeed self-destructive that that person would deprecate their own needs for some larger, perhaps even vague purpose. But this deprecation of personal self-interest in favor of vague outcomes in pursuit of conservative social issues is exactly how many Christian conservatives seem to vote.

It is perhaps the Christian conservative voters' psychological predisposition to faith, belief without evidence, that makes the conservative Christian voter so vulnerable, in many cases willing or even eager to deprecate their own self-interest to vote almost exclusively for candidates who appear (however counter to any evidence of this social agenda support after the fact) to support their social agenda while in office.

It is not a difficult argument to prove that Christian conservatives are often, by large majorities, not compelled to vote for candidates that campaign to improve middle-class finances and stability; for instance improving personal taxes for the middle-class, or improving US job growth, or middle-class income growth.

It is likewise simple to illustrate that Christian conservatives are convincingly compelled in great numbers to vote for the social issues that purport to back their religious faith. What is further stupefying to rationalists, is that conservative Christian voters appear to do both; vote for social issues, and against the very programs that could ensure their families financial health and stability. This is especially difficult to rationalize when those very same politicians who tout these Christian conservative social values during their campaigns, never seem to make any progress toward fulfilling these issues when in office, even when holding rock solid majorities in government.

Bertrand Russell's comments talk of "substituting emotion for evidence", and here too we find compelling potential explanations for Christian conservative voting records. Indeed, most social issues of the conservative Christian are explosively emotional. Think of the strong emotions that come to bear when Christian conservatives discuss abortion, or gay marriage, or gun rights. These issues invoke powerful protective emotions in those who believe these social issues are currently out of whack in our society.

Think back to the narrative of Sarah Palin in 2010. After leaving her elected office as Alaska governor in 2009, Palin toured the country on speaking tours touting her books and firing up the conservative crowds who turned out to see her. Palin's gift is plain-spoken rhetoric that touches the nerve-center of Christian conservative voters. She taps into this with phrases like, "Momma Grizzlies". This invokes images of conservative Christian women, standing like a grizzly bear on their hind legs roaring fiercely to protect her young. A nice image, and at the heart of the emotional Palin appeal to the ideological right.

But what exactly inspires these "Momma Grizzlies" to take this defensive action? Think about it? Is it a direct threat to the financial solvency of their families and therefore a direct threat to their children's future? Not really. No, it's a defensive stance against the "moral decay" of our secular democracy. One would think that the stagnant, even declining incomes of the middle-class in the face of rising cost of living would be a much more direct inspiration for this bear-like metaphor - but no. The main social issues that seem to stimulate this defensive grizzly bear stance, have nothing to do with the welfare of the family's finances - which are under direct threat - it's the much more indirect threat of alternative lifestyles that raises the ire of these GOP faithful voters and inspires this "noble" defensive "momma grizzly" stance.

Personal sacrifice is another base tenant of the Christian faithful. The New Testament speaks endlessly to putting aside your own needs to assist the poor and the downtrodden. Here are a few examples:

> *You will be made rich in every way so that you can be generous on every occasion, and through us your generosity will result in thanksgiving to God (2 Corinthians 9:11).*

> *One man gives freely, yet gains even more; another withholds unduly, but comes to poverty (Proverbs 11:24)*

> *Remember this: Whoever sows sparingly will also reap sparingly, and whoever sows generously will also reap generously (2 Corinthians 9:6)*

It is easy to see that this same mindset of sacrifice of one's own personal security and wealth is so noble in the Christian mindset, that it perhaps sets a trap for politicians to leverage.

Indeed, who can argue that the middle-class Christian has sacrificed their own piece of the American dream so that the wealthy can become ever more so?

That is exactly what has been happening for 30 years via GOP policies, and perhaps this "sacrificial mindset" is part of an explanation as to why Christian conservatives sit idly by as their GOP lawmakers ignore their social and financial needs, focusing all their attention on business and the wealthy, yet still somehow get re-elected.

So, perhaps this predisposition to believe, no matter the evidence, is at the heart of explaining how Christian conservative voters can place such blind and dedicated trust in public officials who talk the talk - even when they never even attempt to walk that walk and back up their rhetoric. Further, perhaps it is some sort of Christian devotion to "noble sacrifice" of personal financial health and stability in favor of nobly pushing relentlessly on vague notions of social moral decay that are at the heart of explaining the self-destructive behavior of US middle-class conservative voters.

Conclusion

This letter to US middle-class Christian voters has been a recap of current and historical events, some disparate, others related and then is followed in every case by an effort to find rational and logical coherence between these events to explain them and to attempt to ferret out the principles that seem to underpin the related actions of GOP legislators.

As always, reasonable people can and will disagree with the conclusions I have drawn.

This is natural.

However, I would ask you; if you find my conclusions less than satisfying then seek your own conclusions with equal care to be rational and objective.

This means emotional conclusions with minimal evidence are less valuable than logical conclusions with ample evidence.

Surely there are many ways to interpret the actions of others, but I believe this book represents a logical construct, built on reasonable conclusions.

While one can never fully know the motives of others with any level of confidence, the actions of our lawmakers - especially when they repeat over and over - are powerful evidence of a motivational principle that underlies and drives the actions of our lawmakers.

Many people, left, center, and right, base their actions on a set of core principles. Guideposts to make sense of complex events and problems, conclude actions within parameters of core principles, and then act accordingly. For the most part, I do not ascribe purposefully destructive motives to the GOP.

I rather point out in their behavior and in the repetitive actions they take, and that within their behavior lie clues to the folly, illogic, and the demonstrable destructive outcomes (intended and unintended) of many of their core principles and the related actions they take.

There are many GOP strategies and actions challenged in this book. Many have unintended, or perhaps intended, consequences that are damaging to our democracy, and particular damaging to the middle-class.

To restate only one:

Conservative principle dictates that the power of free markets must be maintained and nurtured at all costs.

This is not a controversial statement and in and of itself not a bad principle.

However the actions one takes to maintain and nurture our free markets must be made with a full understanding of them. Free markets are not just about business. Indeed, as discussed earlier, free markets are a complex symbiosis between supply (business) and demand (consumers).

Both must be maintained and nurtured for free markets to thrive. Too often the demand-side of this equation is taken for granted, slighted, harmed, and undermined in perhaps a valiant attempt to live up to the core principle that free markets must be protected.

It is also possible that absolute power corrupts absolutely, and a reasonable person must admit that it is possible that willful manipulation of emotional social issues has and is occurring daily to disingenuously enfranchise the weak and underrepresented middle-class to get their votes, simply in a cynical and destructive attempt to gain and retain power.

Clearly special interest power from consumers is almost non-existent in our government, aside from our votes. The same cannot be said for special interest power advocating the wealthy and big-business. These special interest lobbying groups are massive, well-funded, and constantly active. Human nature, and common sense would dictate that even if a lawmaker is aware, committed and believes that healthy free markets means maintaining this supply/demand balance, the daily drumbeat of wealthy business special interest in your ear, your pocket, your career, even in your very existence as a powerful lawmaker would lead you to forget that the quiet, under-represented consumer (demand side) of this equation is just as important and is floundering from your neglect - whether intended or unintended.

If you are a Christian conservative voter, I hope this book has given you pause to consider the power you have at your disposal. You and those who believe like you are reported to be more than one-fourth of the US electorate - a formidable voting block. If you focus your vote and your interests simply on the emotional social issues that stir you - abortion, gay rights, gun rights, God in government, and fighting moral decay in general - you do so at your own peril.
Indeed, by focusing so much interest on emotional social issues, you set yourself up to be manipulated by politicians who piously tell you what you want to hear.

As we have shown, even if they get elected, they almost never really address your social issues. You have wasted your vote, and harmed your family's financial stability, and indirectly harmed the US economy in terrible ways.

As was discussed earlier, tight adherence to ideological frameworks is common, but the real world does not operate on such a basis. Real life is messy and sub-optimal. You simply must focus on more than the social issues that drive you to the polls, and think of what you - as a middle-class consumer - want from your government. What you want for your country. What you want for your family.

As simple as this sounds, it seems to run counter to Christian conservative practices. It is unseemly perhaps for Christians to be so self-interested. But you live in a wealthy country where no one should struggle to thrive, raise healthy and educated children, and give them the ever-improving life and lifestyle you were given by your parents.

A bit more about our parents. They lived in a simpler world. But it was a world that swept social issues under the rug; out of sight, out of mind. Abortions were carried out in back alleys with coat hangers.

In your parent's lifetime, becoming elderly meant almost certain poverty for the vast majority. The presence of homosexuals was something that could almost be thought non-existent - given how these populations, which certainly existed, hid from public view. Sex was not routinely practiced outside the bounds of marriage, it was simply taboo. And on and on. Their world was simpler, and they strove to improve their families, to improve their communities, and to ensure their financial solvency and yours.

Our generation is much more complex. Information travels faster. Once oppressed groups are no longer silent and out of sight and mind. Abortions, while still a tragedy, are an imperfect answer to a daunting problem that will no longer be confined to back alleys, no matter our abhorrence for the practice. Sexual freedom without the need for marriage is no longer taboo, it is commonplace.

If we think of these new realities as all that matters in maintaining our families and our society, we risk the very real destruction of the middle-class, of ourselves, and ultimately of our nation. If that hyper-focus by Christian conservatives on social issues alone is allowed to continue - and it continues even today in a tireless march - the very fiscal foundations that made America so rich will be lost. And recovering it won't be easy.

Our country must once again focus on the common good, on not only loudly advocating for the social issues that echo our core religious beliefs, but also and with equal fervor, forcing our elected officials not to forget the important middle-class.

Business simply cannot exist without a large and healthy middle-class. If we don't stand up for these rights, and put our social issues into the proper priority, we will soon find ourselves living in an only once great nation.

We will lose our lead as a shining light on the hill of freedom, a beacon for the world, and become the world's largest banana republic - with a small class of ultra-wealthy, surrounded by a disaffected class of former middle-class consumers, now struggling simply to exist from one day to the next.

I believe it is our firm and solemn duty to maintain the middle-class who drive the markets we so depend on for our strength, our freedom, and our happiness.

And to make this our *first* priority again.

1 The Last Word, MSNBC -

http://bigjournalism.com/libertychick/2010/11/06/msnbcs-lawrence-

odonnell-proudly-proclaims-i-am-a-socialist/

2 House Tax Proposal Analysis - http://bit.ly/a631UG

3 What The Top U.S. Companies Pay in Taxes, How can it be that you pay

more to the IRS than General Electric? http://bit.ly/bQrGNX

4 Slate Magazine - http://www.slate.com/id/2266025/entry/2266026

5 Our Banana Republic - http://nyti.ms/c14DBZ

6 Daily Kos Blog -   http://www.dailykos.com/story/2011/02/23/948023/-

New-CBO-estimate-on-Affordable-Care-Act-and-deficits

7 USA Today - http://usat.ly/cYDPqb

8 NY Times - http://nyti.ms/bHTdkf

10 Center for American Progress - http://bit.ly/9ghsDV

11 NY Times - http://bit.ly/fszMJo

12 NY Times - http://nyti.ms/ij23oS

13 The Rachel Maddow Show, MSNBC - http://exm.nr/hrzd3I

14 Wikipedia - http://en.wikipedia.org/wiki/History_of_the_Internet

15 Fiscal Strength - http://www.fiscalstrength.com/

16 The Nation Magazine -

http://www.thenation.com/blog/156569/patriotic-millionaires-explain-tax-

cuts-rich-dont-grow-economy

17 Wikipedia - http://en.wikipedia.org/wiki/New_Deal

18 Wikipedia - http://en.wikipedia.org/wiki/The_Southern_strategy

19 Politifact - http://politifact.com/truth-o-meter/promises/obameter/rulings/promise-kept/

20 Demand Side - http://www.demandsideeconomics.net/

21 Amazon - http://www.amazon.com/exec/obidos/ASIN/1591841917/reasonmagazine

22 Wikipedia - http://en.wikipedia.org/wiki/Adam_Smith

23 New Yorker Magazine - http://www.newyorker.com/reporting/2010/08/30/100830fa_fact_mayer

24 NY Times - http://www.nytimes.com/2010/08/29/opinion/29rich.html

25 Amazon - http://www.amazon.com/Most-Human-Talking-Computers-Teaches/dp/0385533063

26 C-Span - http://www.c-span.org/Events/Iowa-Conservatives-Hosts-GOP-Presidential-Hopefuls/10737420004/

27 Associated Press International - http://www.wlns.com/Global/story.asp?S=14220037

28 Palm Beach Post - http://www.palmbeachpost.com/news/state/gov-rick-scotts-proposed-education-budget-1-75-1302720.html

29 Washington Independent - http://washingtonindependent.com/91632/companies-sitting-on-cash-but-not-hiring

30 Money News - http://www.moneynews.com/FinanceNews/Bernanke-GOP-Budget-Cuts/2011/03/03/id/388164

31 House.gov - http://majorityleader.house.gov/newsroom/2011/02/leader-cantor-on-the-latest-unemployment-report-we-must-cut-spending-to-grow-jobs.html

32 H.R.1 - http://www.govtrack.us/congress/bill.xpd?bill=h112-1

33 GovTrack.US - http://www.govtrack.us/congress/bill.xpd?bill=h112-2

34 GovTrack.US - http://www.govtrack.us/congress/bill.xpd?bill=h112-3

35 Wikipedia - http://en.wikipedia.org/wiki/Faith

Follow Daniel Burgin's book blog at:

Someonelied.blogspot.com

Follow Daniel Burgin on Twitter at:

@ChristianVoters

Follow Daniel Burgin on Facebook at:

http://on.fb.me/gjIC4K

Watch for Daniel Burgin's new political book

The Conservative Psyche

coming in the summer of 2011